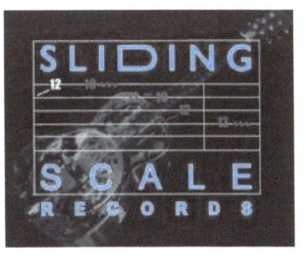

slidingscale.co.uk

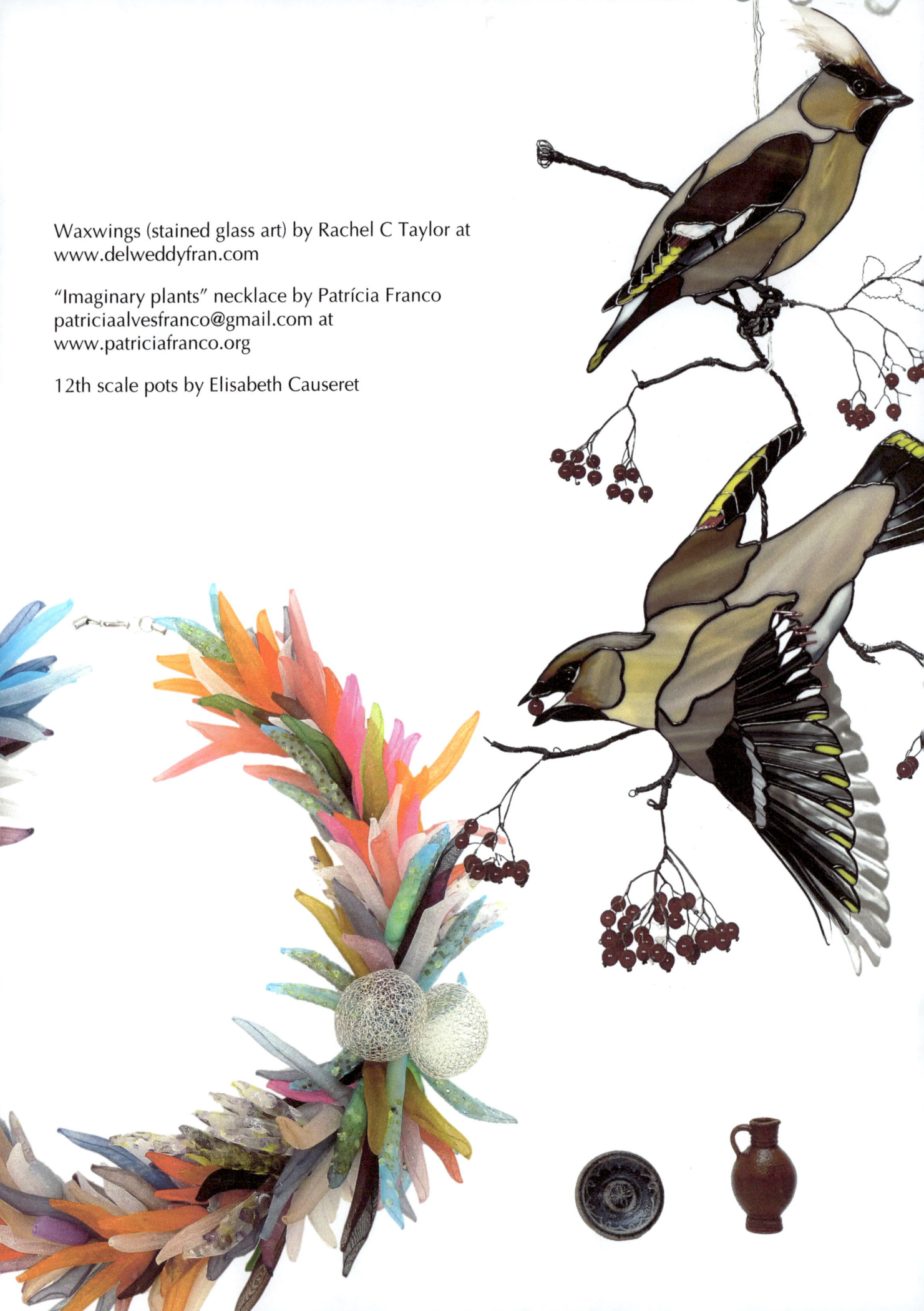

Waxwings (stained glass art) by Rachel C Taylor at www.delweddyfran.com

"Imaginary plants" necklace by Patrícia Franco patriciaalvesfranco@gmail.com at www.patriciafranco.org

12th scale pots by Elisabeth Causeret

"Knitting Nanna" (approx 1cm) by Alicia Graciela Volta (AligraDolls) www.etsy.com/shop/AligraDolls

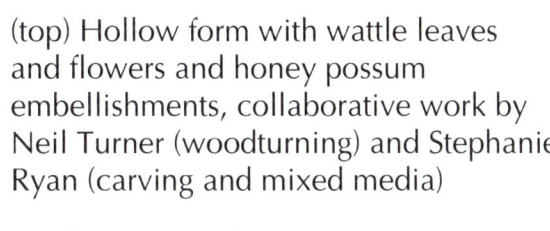

Rocking horse SVG 12th scale for Cricut by Lisa Sones-Peck www.spellboundminiatures.com

Crochet Columbo by Katrina Stiff at snorkers.art

(top) Hollow form with wattle leaves and flowers and honey possum embellishments, collaborative work by Neil Turner (woodturning) and Stephanie Ryan (carving and mixed media)

Sunflowers SVG by Angie & Frank www.etsy.com/shop/AngieScarrCrafts

"Working in miniature from Angie's book" miniature display 12th scale by Nathalie Gireaud www.provenceminiatures.fr

Dedication

Dedicated to all my Patreon patrons, both those who are listed on the thanks page and the anonymous ones. Without you this book would never have seen the light of day. Thank you.

Publishing Data

First edition published 2023 (SSPB15)

Text copyright Angie Scarr and Frank Fisher

Illustration, composites and photographs copyright Frank Fisher and Angie Scarr

Design by Frank Fisher and Angie Scarr

Sliding Scale, Plaza De Andalucía 1, Campofrío, 21668, Huelva, Spain.

ISBN 9788412602326

All rights reserved. No part of this book may be reproduced, or transmitted in any form or by any means without the express permission of the copyright owners.

The right of Angie Scarr and Frank Fisher to be identified as the author of this work has been asserted in accordance with the Copyright Designs and Patents Act 1988, sections 77 & 78.

No part of this publication may be reproduced, stored in a retrieval system or transmitted in any form or by any means without the prior permission of the publisher and author or their agents.

Descriptions of sales and advertising platforms are for information purposes only and are not recommendations. The authors can accept no responsibility for the application of any information contained in this book. Further, no responsibility is implied or accepted for current or future application of social media and data collection laws.

The publishers and author can accept no legal responsibility for any consequences arising from the application of information instructions or advice given in this publication.

Contents

Introduction	7
Why we self-publish	8
100 day challenges	8
The cons and pros of self-publishing	9
Self-publishing companies and "hybrid" publishers	11

Part 1: Plan (and research) — 12

Planning (and starting to write notes)	12
Anti-planning	12
Researching your own motivations	13
Who is your audience?	14
See if you can create a personality	14
Be the best you can	15
Writing style	15

Part 2: Get Serious — 17

Write (and photograph)	17
Get a plan - the first plan	17
Your first page planner	20
Get moving on the projects or sections	20
Where am I going to keep my work and backups?	21
Your readers' problems are your problems	22
How to use your 100 day planner	23

Part 3: Photography — 26

Backgrounds	26
Image resolution	27
Lighting	27
Process shots (step-by-steps)	29

Part 4: Carrying on writing — 30

How best to start your writer's day	30
The dynamics of your book	31
How do you choose to put your project together?	32
What to do with procrastination	33
What can you do?	33
Refining your style	34

Part 5: Marketing strategy — 36

Researching and planning	36
Secrecy ... and openness	38
Marketing and positioning problem	39
Get your customers ready	41

Part 6: Preparing your work for publishing — 43

Are you ready to start editing?	43
American English vs British English?	44
Front and end matter	44
Self-publish with assistance, or find a publisher?	45
Editing and other Author Services	46
First thoughts on pricing	47

Part 7: Pre-publication strategies — 48

Title and design of your book cover	48
How a subtitle can help you sell a book	48
Choosing Categories and Keywords	48
"Hot launch"	50
Description	52

Part 8: Putting the book together — 53

Photo editing	53
Layout	56
Chapter structure and multiple files	56
Inner layout design	57
Sectional text flow	61
Photo text flow	62
Contents	64
Index	64
Advertising pages	65
ISBNs	66
Cover design	67
First, bad cover design	67
Our first cover concepts	68

Part 9: The publishing process — 73

Upload — 73
Backup — 75
Amazon versus Ingram — 75
Proof copies — 76
Publish your book just before payday! — 76
Ebook — 77

Part 10: Post publication marketing — 80

Make a marketing strategy — 80
Watch your sales appear on KDP — 82
Unusual activity — 83
Backing up your books with video — 83
Check your Amazon rankings — 84
Requesting extra categories — 84

Amazon Ads — 86

The dark arts of advertising — 86
Glossary of terms — 86
How to set up your ads — 87
Automatic or manual targeting — 88
Product or keyword targeting — 88
Expensive search terms/product targets — 89
Cheaper advertising — 89
Launch campaign — 91
Keep an eye on your ads — 91
Advertising leading to sales elsewhere — 92
How to come back from a cold launch — 92

Biography — 94

Thanks and acknowledgements — 94

Patreon - Why I love my patrons — 95

Other books by Sliding Scale — 96

Index — 97

Introduction

We noticed that, although there are lots of books on the market about self-publishing there weren't any specifically to help craft, hobby and DIY writers to get from first ideas to a finished book on a limited budget.

Crafters may want to produce a book in order to add that book to their business assets both in order to add to the authority of their brand, and as one 'trickle' of a multiple income stream.

If you think you will make a lot of money from your first book, whether self-published or traditionally published, you're probably wrong. My first and second books were both traditionally published and, although they have both been bestsellers in their field my income level was not spectacular in the first years.

We do know people who have had the experience of earning big or relatively big within months. They are few and far between and hit the market first with a very new idea at the time. We can all dream, though! To be more realistic, your first book should form part of a multiple income strategy. You will have to invest a large chunk of time (I would estimate a minimum of 100 days part time) into it, for uncertain rewards. And your book could go straight in at number one in its niche. The magic number to start to see real income from books or indeed videos and other media seems to me to be 3. Have I put you off yet? No? Then continue reading because you can get a big selling first book or you can build on minor successes to build a greater one. All these goals are best achieved by putting the best possible product on to the market, if possible, in a new and potentially popular niche, and marketing really well both before and after publication.

If you want to do it enough and feel you have something people are going to want to read, you're probably right.

The best way of thinking of your first book is to see it simply as part of your whole business plan. Producing a book is stamping your authority on your niche and making your work pay you more than once. Often your craft books will explore your old tutorials in depth, or create new teaching opportunities. Frank and I have published, off the top of my head, 15 books so far. We've also helped several others with support and advice. Sometimes we haven't given advice that we know people really need because it isn't always graciously received. Sometimes we've decided to bite the bullet and tell a dear friend that something could be improved. Having said this OUR work would always have been greatly improved by the use of a thorough editor.

Unfortunately we have never been able to afford one. Similarly marketing has been a learning curve and we are continuing to learn. There are many titles out there which cover marketing more extensively. We just get you started here. We give some advice about what to do to rescue a poor launch since we've learned from our own flops too.

In this book, I cover writing and marketing tips, while my husband and self-publishing partner Frank delves into the technical aspects of laying out and publishing your book.

It is highly recommended that you use an editor, as it minimises the risk of embarrassing mistakes. However if your financial status means that's not an option, don't let it discourage you from writing and publishing your own book. Similarly if you can't afford a cover designer there are some tips to help you not to fall into the black hole of obscurity merely by having an ugly cover.

If you've ever thought of writing your own craft book, hobby, or DIY book, or a self-help book with a creative edge you're going to get an idea of how tough it can be, but also how exciting. For me the process has always been like everything else I do … step-by-step and stumble-by-stumble. I have made plenty of mistakes which I share candidly with you. After all, none of us are born experts and our mistakes are often what make us more able to share our personal experience and better methods.

Throughout this book I will always discuss the cheapest way of doing everything because that is our experience. We have self-published at almost zero monetary cost throughout just because we started our business lives again 6 years ago after an illness and with almost nothing. However, these cheaper or cost free methods may not be the most efficient, so feel free to use writing, design or layout software that works better for you. If outsourcing help with photography, editing, publishing, or marketing makes the process easier, quicker, or more efficient for you, and you can afford it, go for it! I do however want to stress again that lack of funds should be no barrier to self publishing, if you have an idea worth sharing.

Why we self-publish

Being an author is never about big money immediately. We need to be clear about that. It's about investing in your future, a delayed gratification. Personally, I'm investing in my future retirement by writing now. I figured that since my first book has been selling for 20 years and counting, I should, if I make it, be receiving a trickle income right into my 80s from the books we've already published.

I'm not writing from the point of view of a million-selling independent author. However, after 6 productive years during which almost all my self-published books were born, I can now say that more than a third of our income comes from book sales. This is almost double last year, which is almost double the year before. I'm aiming to increase it again next year. In the following years, I want to maintain my position by writing one or two books a year in different genres.

If you aren't sure, start with a few written or video tutorials. No time is wasted doing these first, as they can form the foundation of your books. Or, you can sell tutorials as PDFs, live or video classes.

100 day challenges

Several times over the last few years I have given myself 100 day challenges in order to give impetus and self discipline to a project. In every case this challenge has given rise to at least one book. In one case it gave rise to two, as during the writing of mine and Kira's Your Creative Business book, I was explaining my writing process to my patrons. This formed notes which went on to form a large chunk of the work towards this book. I know that a book can be written and published within 100 days, even part time, because we've done it. You may wish to take a slower approach. The main thing is to have some form of framework when you do decide definitively that you want to publish a book. Otherwise your project will get shelved. You can of course have several projects on the go at any one time (I do) but only having an end date in mind will give you enough discipline to actually complete and to press on through the days when you really need motivation.

You can choose to read this book cover to cover, all at once and then go back to the bits you need. Or you can use it as a prompt whenever you need one.

If you are already sure you want to go ahead you can go straight to "How to use your 100 day planner" on page 23 with its time planners on the subsequent pages. Decide on a timetable, before reading this book, which will prompt you on your writing journey.

The cons and pros of self-publishing over traditional publications.

Cons:

When you are self-publishing, you bear all the responsibility for the content, quality, and marketing of the product. All the costs of editing, any cover or layout design. There is no help from editors without paying for it.

What you are paying for by having a lower income per book is the greater experience of the publishing houses and therefore an almost guaranteed great product and greater book sales. They have experience in what sells and what doesn't. They are likely to choose better titles and better cover art because of that experience. They have their own skilled marketing departments with all the important marketing links. They attend book fairs so will get your book seen by all the bookshops and the buyers and can raise income from licensing agreements.

Pros:

All this costs them money and so they need to know that your book will sell and make them most of the money. Because of that risk they will push your royalties down as low as they possibly can. On the other hand when self-publishing you will receive all the royalties, and you are in control of what those are, since you decide the price.

You will be in control of speed and efficiency of publication. No arguments with editors over the use of simulate vs emulate (I was correct). No having to ask the publishers every year to stop delaying and cough up your small but important royalties. You have all the artistic control. You can be really up to date even innovative with your approach if you don't even know the 'rules'. Sometimes this can result in a better, more exciting book.

So, your sales numbers will almost definitely be lower when self-publishing but your income may be much higher.

My personal experience of being traditionally published has its ups and downs. Ups because I knew I had a good idea and, fortunately, so did the publisher, so they accepted my synopsis immediately and offered me a contract very quickly. There were some minor hiccups along the way but overall my experience of the publishing company was very good. However, at the end, the major problem became that I'd signed a contract without fully understanding the implications of the words "selling price". I assumed I'd be earning 10% of the cover price (a foolish mistake). Would I still have signed? Yes, but I think I would have also noted how low that selling price could go. I'd have seen how my royalty almost always dropped from 10% to 5%, and the tricky way they seemed to engineer that and I would have made sure we had those practises ironed out. I'd have discussed some other sneaky tricks, like giving your book away as a loss leader to sell other books. I did make sure that never happened with my second book. Finally, I would have made sure the author purchase price was as low as the price Amazon was paying. If I had noticed and sorted these inequities earlier, maybe I would still be traditionally published.

Although this book is about self-publishing, if in the end you decide you would benefit more by being traditionally published, there is nothing to stop you changing tack. But do the maths. After two books, when I tried to negotiate a more equitable deal, we couldn't agree.

	Upfront costs	# 7 hr days worked	value per hour	your input	profit per book	# sales to break even
Self publishing Your responsibilities	200 *Writing, photography, editing, layout, marketing*	100	15	10500	4.00	2675
Publishing company Your responsibilities	-1000 *Writing, optionally photography*	60	15	6300	0.20	31500
Publishing services Your responsibilities	4000 *Writing, photography, marketing*	80	15	8400	4.00	3100

How many book sales will it take to cover what I could have earned at an average job?

	Upfront costs	# 7 hr days worked	value per hour	your input	profit per book	# sales to break even
Self publishing Your responsibilities	200 *Writing, photography, editing, layout, marketing*	100	20	14000	4.00	3550
Publishing company Your responsibilities	-1000 *Writing, optionally photography*	60	20	8400	0.20	42000
Publishing services Your responsibilities	4000 *Writing, photography, marketing*	80	20	11200	4.00	3800

How many book sales will it take to cover what I could have earned at a better than average job?

It turns out that not being able to agree is the best way of getting out of a contract. You offer your next book to your publisher at more favourable terms to yourself. If you can't agree - you're free. You're in a very good negotiating position if you already have the confidence to self-publish by knowing the ropes in advance.

If I'd published my own first book, with the number of pre-sales I already had when it was published, it would have been an instant bestseller in its field anyway. However, in those days, self-publishing was a very difficult route to go down.

It was still quite difficult when we first self published my Colour Book, because print on demand wasn't quite yet a 'thing'. As soon as it was, we were ready to go. It was as if we'd been waiting for that all our lives!

With the maturing of the self-pub market and a few clever marketing tricks plus a bit of luck and a good wind in your favour it's still perfectly possible to get a self-published bestseller.

Later in the book I'll share those marketing hacks which I've learned along the way. However, the market is constantly changing and as one trick gets learned and over-used you have to be more and more creative.

The very best thing you can do to ensure success is to write a really good and inspiring craft book and find your 'megafan' customers good and early in the process. They will help you through from publication to good book sales and great reviews, so cherish every single one.

Surprisingly the costs seem to be similar whether you publish yourself or with publishing services added, but to pay for services you have to find the money up front. Whereas when you self-publish you only have to front the time. I also noted that the number that came out for the publishing company in the second example happened to be very similar to the numbers of each book actually sold by my publishing company over ten years or more (they continue to sell). In fact we did make more money by selling our books at live events. It is worth mentioning that these were and always have been best sellers. Although I am often disparaging about publishing contracts the publishers did a very good job of promotion and I may not have been as well known had it not been for their input. They picked me up because I had existing videos and a good synopsis.

Self-publishing companies and "hybrid" publishers

An early warning: don't be conned by a so-called self-publisher company, which is actually an expensive author services company. Some of them are good, but there is way too much 'sharp practice' going on where companies target the ego and insecurity of the writer. Many of us just want to be published the first time round and make mistakes. We sign on the dotted line without thinking. This is dangerous, as we can make bad decisions on contracts with a traditional publisher, with a hybrid company, or even get scammed by less-than-scrupulous 'publishers'. Our desire to see our book in print can override our judgement, as can the desire to publish regardless of the market.

If a company wants to publish your book but asks you to pay for publication, you aren't talking to a traditional publisher. It's as simple as that. If you have plenty of money and just want to see a professional looking book, you can go that route, but "buyer beware!" You can individually buy all the services one of these companies offer, often at a more equitable and transparent price. I am unpopular with these companies for saying this, especially with those who are the least transparent and don't like people warning against them.

Of course, there are probably good companies who can take away all your stress if your project is a 'vanity book'. That is, you just want to be published and don't care if your book costs more than it earns. Expect to spend several thousands of pounds/dollars/euros. If your book is really that good a concept but you don't want the stress of self-publishing, a traditional publisher is the way to go.

We will talk later about individual publishing help services that you can, and often should, contract individually.

Part 1: Plan (and research)

Here are the processes you should consider when deciding to write a craft book, or to pull one together from various pieces of work you already have.

1. **Plan**
   and start writing
2. **Write & gather images**
   and continue planning
3. **Edit**
   and continue writing perhaps for a second book
4. **Market**
   start as soon as it really looks like it will be a book
5. **Design**
   prepare for how you want your book to look
6. **Layout**
   the pulling together of your text and pictures into a book
7. **Upload proof**
   scary and exciting but not as difficult as you might think
8. **Hit publish**
   wow! Tell everyone & celebrate
9. **Market**
   again. This is VERY important

Planning (and starting to write notes)

"Will I be able to write a book?"

If you have ever taught your craft, if you have ever put together a magazine article, if you love to read. If you enjoy showing other people how to achieve the results that you achieve, you can write a book. If you can take lovely photographs already, it will help but there is information on this a little later. If you love sharing inspiration, you will be a great craft or creativity author.

If you are terrified of people copying your work you will have real difficulty being a craft author. I believe a good craft book relies on very open, honest and generous sharing of information.

If you want to write a book but don't yet know what subject you would like to cover, start taking notes along with everything you do and you can pick from them later. You will probably be taking pictures for your sales and marketing anyway, so now start taking photographs of your processes too.

If you're starting immediately, please take a look at the photography and photographic equipment sections as soon as possible so you don't even waste one of your hours.

Anti-planning

You don't need to start with serious planning if it doesn't come naturally to you. If you are already in the middle of a project that is taking up most of your time and you just feel that getting it down on paper and in photographs is the most important thing; then go right ahead. The important thing is that writing fits in with your creative life at this stage, and not the other way round. This can change, though, and one day you might find that you are a writer first and a crafter/DIYer second. But for now let's assume that you have a craft that you feel relatively experienced or innovative enough to write about. As described in my 'Your Creative Business' book, writing and teaching your work can form one of several serious multiple income streams, which you can build on to future-proof your business. So, while you're working at your 'day job', it makes sense to keep notes and photographs throughout, even if you think your book is a long way down the line. If you aren't planning on a 100 day challenge, it could be at least a year before you have enough material to put together. Then at the end you'll need to add a little more of your time to make a viable book.

> So, if you want to write a book, start straight away even if it's in a very informal way. Grab a notebook or start a Google Doc or voice to text; whatever feels comfortable. Just take notes whenever something occurs to you. Don't be afraid to experiment even if you have never written more than an email before.

Read through at least the sections on writing and photographing your work so that you have some idea of your why, your who and your how. That will save time later. Why you might be writing a book, who you would be writing it for and how you will proceed. Your method or style will help you decide what photographs and notes to take. If you want to develop a chatty style, it helps to write down little anecdotes, like where things went wrong or where inspiration hit. This can also help for troubleshooting sections. After all, we all start as beginners and your mistakes are what made you an expert. Your ideal reader is buying the ability to bypass those mistakes and will often enjoy your story about the uncomfortable mistakes they can now skip.

Before you even start deciding to formalise writing a book you should collect all your ideas. These notes are not just for your first book but anything that pops up as a good idea for later or for another use. Write it down as you are sure to lose it later otherwise. If it still looks like a good idea down the line; it probably is a good idea.

Takeaway
Never let an idea go to waste and never do anything just for one purpose. You can multiply your income by repurposing your learning, teaching and researching.

Researching your own motivations - Your why, what and who

If you have time to plan, and you're now serious about the project, these are the first questions you will ask yourself. You can come back to them over and over again to make sure you're fulfilling a brief. Also, if you do decide to go the publisher route, the planning will form part of your synopsis. So let's look at those questions.

Why do you want to publish a book? Fame, fortune or a sense of achievement. I rather hope you've straight away answered "all three" even though the first two don't arrive magically as soon as you hit publish; the last one certainly does. That sense of achievement is addictive too. I can say from experience that you never get over the thrill of getting your newly published book in your hands. My thrill is just as great with my 15th self-published book as it was with my first traditionally published book. It might seem as if you would write the same book whichever of these reasons is uppermost in your mind, but equally you may take a different route or make different decisions if money is your main incentive. You might wish to write more, shorter books, depending on what your customer requires. You could choose subjects that are more popular if income is your main reason, or more niche if you want the sense of achievement and you are the most knowledgeable person in your specialty.

> What do you have to add that hasn't been said before or hasn't been gathered together in that way before?

What is the subject of your proposed book, if you know yet. Can you give it a working title and some possible subtitles? You can keep adding to these ideas as more come to you. What does the work teach? You can change the title later after doing a bit of keyword research. One of the best ways of pinning down your theme is to give it a title. This should not be your final title even if you know it. Keep that one secret!

What are you going to use to keep your notes or start writing seriously? Will it be a notebook? Will it be digital documents or will it be some kind of specialist writer software?

The cheapest way is simply to start off using Google Docs. This gives you the ability to make side notes, to share your document with others and to make sure it's always saved even if the power goes off. That being said, always back up your work. I back up to an ODT document at the end of every session whenever I've made significant changes.

My husband then backs up my whole machine to his. You could simply send finished drafts as documents to a friend or friends who you trust just to make sure if you do lose a document that there's always a copy.

If you have difficulty in thinking about a whole book, start with a tutorial and then keep adding more tutorials until you have the bones of a book. Your working title might simply be your name "Ellen Fisher's knitting book", for example.

I always have several book docs on the go at any one time.

Who is your audience?

Here are a few questions to ask yourself. Who is my audience? In a craft book your audience will probably be very much people like you, with just a little less confidence. Who is your ideal reader? Why did they pick your book up, or these days more likely choose it on Amazon?

Here's one of my ideal readers of my craft books: She's around 40. Let's call her Millie. Her kids are in school. She works, but not full time she really wants to start a craft business on the side. Maybe she already has. She's had some ups and downs and is a little under confident. She likes lots of illustrations because she is a very visual learner and other people's ideas easily inspire her own. She has always loved everything tiny and colourful and perfect and she can be a bit of a relaxed perfectionist herself. She's dabbled in lots of crafts but is always drawn back to miniatures. She has a crafting space or room and tends to collect materials and books.

See if you can create a personality for your reader

For this "author book" my readers are much more diverse, so I have several of them. Millie is still there of course, because she's moved on from learning to create to being an expert herself. Now her kids are in high school, and she's sick of working for a demanding boss. She quite fancies writing a book about a new technique she's invented!

I'd also like to appeal to Scott. He's an illustrator and wants to write a book about illustrating children's books. He has a child of six and one of ten, so he not only knows how to illustrate but he also knows what appeals to very young, and a little older, children.

It really helps me to have these reader profiles, especially for this book, which reaches outside my miniatures readers and into my Your Creative Business readers.

You really need to continue to think about your audience as you're writing. It's no good using pompous language for a child's book. It's also important that you think about what kind of a book you're aiming to produce. Is it intended to be a very informative and serious textbook, or light hearted and entertaining? I think if you take yourself too seriously you might end up writing a university level document for a class of seven year olds. That's an exaggeration, of course, but If you get that wrong it can be very expensive.

A few years ago a friend put together a how-to book for a new, little-known craft. Their background in education led them towards a preference for textbook style writing and production.

It was too late to warn them because the publishing wheels were already in motion. As soon as I saw the proof, I could see problems. Maybe it was a good book but it was weighty and expensive for a market that hardly existed in Europe at the time, and as a result it simply didn't sell. It was just the wrong book for the market as it existed then. My friend's mistake was to be so keen to be first to market that they were afraid of asking for evaluation and advice. The original book was "hybrid" published I believe. It wouldn't necessarily be in the publisher's interests, as they saw them, to warn that it was an unsellable product. Eventually, we had the conversations about it and now they are self-publishing books that will sell at a more appropriate size and price level for the market. They are getting the buzz of holding more publications in their hands and hopefully gaining more sales. If they want to re-release the original book to a more mature market, they can still do that. Or they can cut it down into smaller part-works.

It's very common and understandable to be afraid that someone will beat you to the market with a similar title. In reality this is rarely the case and stylistically everyone is different. Do ask a friend or three to give you honest critique on your book contents and in fact the cover too. We are rarely direct with people about poor covers as criticism is not usually appreciated, but sometimes we do show a friend a possible alternative. Do ask a sample of your audience. Don't just ask your friends. You know they will be too kind. Ask the ones you can guarantee won't just tell you what they think you want to hear.

Takeaway
Your audience should dictate your style and tone. A book teaching children to knit will have quite a different tone and style to a book teaching complex woodcarving to adults.

Be the best you can

Are you confident that people are interested in your work? When I say "your work", I don't necessarily mean your artistic creations themselves. I mean that you need to be confident that your book will have something that sets it apart from others in the field or adds something to the sum of knowledge on that subject, or is simply more attractive, easier to read or just more fun to read and follow. That doesn't even mean that it has to be the best writing, the most comprehensive work, etc. It simply needs to meet a need that either hasn't been dealt with before. Or that you think you can cover in a way that one introduces the subject more clearly to beginners, or goes further into a theme, or simply looks more attractive to the buyer. I think competition is healthy. When releasing a book with a similar theme to another, it's crucial to identify your Unique Selling Point (USP). Your book could be more detailed, more colourful, more inspirational or aimed at another age group.

Will people buy your book even if they have already bought another book on the same subject? Generally the answer is yes. For example I buy every book I can find on living in Spain and have several books on walking the Camino de Santiago. The subjects are the same, but the treatment is different in each case.

Writing style

You can also start to address style at this stage of your planning. Your writing style may be authoritative, enthusiastic, inspirational or confidential or a mixture of all these and many more.

Is it matter-of-fact, simply informative, or chatty? It's easier to make a craft book than a novel from this point of view since you can construct your text simply as a series of captions on photographs so if you don't have a writing style it really doesn't matter for producing a simple step-by-step projects book. Having said that, remember your ideal customer. What is going to make her/him happy?

The thing about writing a book and setting yourself up as an expert is that once your knowledge is out there, it's out there. And if you are wrong, it will come back to bite you. Make sure that at least your information is correct if you present it as fact. In a more informal, chattier style book you can say "I'm not sure how this will work out".

Don't try to be too authoritative in a new area, especially if you really don't know everything about your subject, and to be honest, which of us do? You don't need an over-abundance of authority to inspire. Just natural and contagious enthusiasm.

Most of my books, but not all, are step-by-step. Step-by-step is great for individual projects but you can also inspire by simply explaining theories and showing illustrations where you want the reader to come up with their own ideas. You can find language that makes them dream and imagine. They will then be encouraged to try the easy steps. Ultimately you want them to be confident that they can go on to think of their own designs.

Keep the reader informed in advance of any difficulties. This is where taking notes can help while you are working. It's so easy to forget where you yourself got tripped up once you've done something successfully. Your book buyer is paying for a shortcut through those mistakes. Always remember that your job is not to swan around being cleverer than your reader, but to get right in into their workspace with them. Amuse, entertain, encourage, reassure and inspire them. It's not all about you. It's about their experience. I can't stress that enough.

Let me give you a little metaphor. Have you ever been to a gig where the most accomplished musician leaves you with an unsatisfied feeling because you feel she was playing for him/herself? On the flip side, what about those gigs where the musician makes you feel they are playing or singing just for you? Spine tingling isn't it?

The pinnacle of inspiration is when you have the audience really believing in themselves. Because you believe in them. You don't have to be the best writer in the world. You just have to look at the problem through their eyes and from a humble point of view. Often your reader is fearful of making the first step. They need to know that you, their teacher, have fallen and that falling is a good thing when you're learning; especially when you're inventing. Don't forget either, that many of your readers will go on to be better at or have a greater knowledge of your subject than you. If that doesn't keep you humble but also proud … nothing will.

One more thing. If that last image scared you, please don't write a book. You will be sharing knowledge that other people will improve on and leave you creatively in their dust. You have to want to see people fly higher than you have. You have to want to share your secrets and make them theirs. Oftentimes they won't even acknowledge their start with your teaching, and you have to be somewhat OK with that, because it happens.

Well, those are my feelings on style but if you disagree that's good too, because you'll be producing your own book in your own style.

Takeaway
Your reader rarely wants to know how much better at the subject you are than them. What they really want to do is emulate your success!

Part 2: Get Serious

Write (and photograph)

General principles of planning and doing

Let's assume that you've decided you are ready to start writing your book. What should you do first?

Get an idea - make a plan, get started, add & remove ideas, change the plan. Stay flexible.

Some people think planning can hold you back or they get distressed if the plan doesn't work. A plan is a loose framework you can hang bits of the project on. It's up to you how self disciplined you are and having a plan should never mean you can't change the plan. I've even changed which book I'm going to finish first in the middle of a plan!

Following very strict rules can make you uncreative, but having a relaxed guideline can help you hang your ideas together. Later having a deadline is more important and becomes imperative as you get further through the process.

> Having a plan does not stop you collecting ideas for other books while you're working on your first one; it stops you wasting hundreds of hours without achieving anything.

Think step-by-step and don't get disheartened when you get a setback. As long as your general impetus is forwards.

Get a plan - the first plan

Don't know where to start? What do you know? What material (work/writing/photographs) have you already got? What do people know you for? What do you feel passionate about? What do you want to explore? What subjects will make you jump out of bed in the morning every morning for 3 months?

Share the beginning of your journey with trusted friends to give you impetus. Tell a friend or a Patreon group or a social media group you created for the project. Having someone to report back to helps you to keep moving forward.

Now look at the general scope of your book. Would it divide neatly into sections? Don't worry if you don't know that yet, but if you already have that idea, you are already further on your way than you think. Write everything down. The daft ideas and the good ideas will come together, and you'll have to mine them later ... for gold.

You can work two ways. You can just start to work on collecting great photos while you are making and inventing. This is my normal method. When I get to the stage where It looks like I have the bones of the book, I then set a publication date a way ahead. Usually 2-3 months. Remember, as soon as you set your publication date, if you stick to it a lot of your work must be directed towards producing the book. It is perfectly possible to produce a book in 100 days (just over 3 months). Remember, though, that's 3 months during which you will not be able to produce much in the way of saleable stock. You will probably make some wonderful pieces. However generally it's not wise to sell them until you are sure you have all the photographs you need, including your front cover photographs. Since most people can't get by with 3 unpaid months, you have to be sure you have enough stock on the shelves before setting your publication date. Or make sure you have another income coming in that will tide you over. If you are already on a low income It can help to plan to be ultra frugal during this time. My book The Frugalist (under the pen name Littleoldladywho) can help with this.

Page planner page 1 - available for download from www.angiescarr.com/blog

inside cover	1	2	3	4	5	6	7	8	9
10	11	12	13	14	15	16	17	18	19
20	21	22	23	24	25	26	27	28	29
30	31	32	33	34	35	36	37	38	39
40	41	42	43	44	45	46	47	48	49
50	51	52	53	54	55	56	57	58	59

Small craft book

Page planner page 2

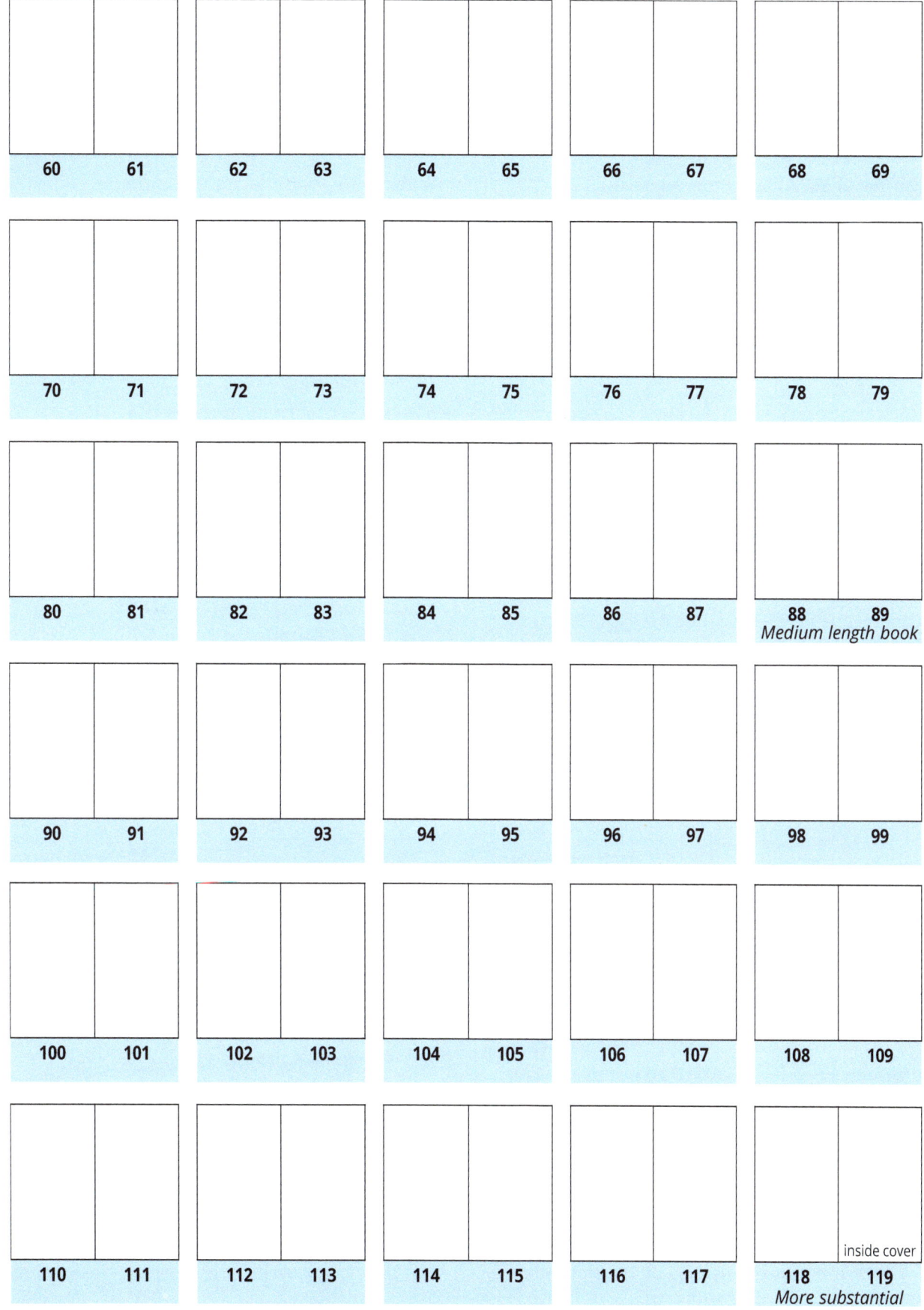

Medium length book

inside cover

More substantial

Your first page planner

Look at the projects you want to put in your book and ask yourself why each of them means something to you. Also ask if they are also connected ideas in any other ways. Write a couple of succinct sentences about each item you're thinking of including (even those you have never made yet) saying why they are included in the book. You might or might not use this work in your book itself but it will help you create a flow of ideas. You may even realise that one item comes naturally after another.

For example my first book was about making four different miniature market stalls. I had to divide the themes into 4 and also make sure there was a flow from easy to more complex ideas. I needed to choose what miniature items would go in each of my stalls according to their difficulty. When working out the techniques I wanted to introduce it became clear that the bread and cakes stall was going to have the simplest polymer clay techniques in, so that obviously went first. Try to introduce ideas slowly, exploring them fully in at least one project before moving on to the next stage.

Scribble your first trial page planner. Photocopy the one on the previous pages, or download a copy from **angiescarr.com/blog** Don't worry about it looking a bit scrappy, too long or too short. That really doesn't matter at this stage. For a longer book add more planner pages.

Remember to block out pages 1-6 for "front matter" and the last handful of pages of your book for end matter. Start using a pencil. It might also help, if you're going to have major sections, to block out some right-hand pages. These could be title pages to a section. If you want to do section titles but find you finish the previous section on a right hand page, the next left hand one can be empty, or have lovely illustrations or photographs on.

Once you have an idea of how you will fill the book, if you like to have a physical manifestation of your work, get a ring binder. Put at least 50 plastic sheets in it. Number the sheets from 1 on the right-hand side then turn the page and put 2 on the left-hand side. The right-hand side sheets are always odd.

Your introduction is likely to start on approximately page 7. This is because before your introduction comes what is called "front matter".

Write your first draft introduction. It will probably be terrible, but don't worry. Just ramble on about why you're writing this book. What led you to this point and what you want to achieve. Put all your hopes and fears in if you want. Write very freely without trying to be too clever. All you're doing is flexing your writing muscles by putting together a page or two of all the thoughts you've had so far today. Put it in your ring binder right around page 7 and maybe 8 too ... for now. Ignore the fact that many publisher books don't number front matter. This is more for you than for the public. It's more a manifesto than an introduction, and it's just to get you exercised and to break the fear of writing.

> Most people write the intro as one of their last tasks at the end of the book but I find it helps to write it twice. This is more for you than for public consumption. However, if you do write in a very free-flowing way it is pretty likely that your passion for your subject will come over and you may well end up using some of the excitable language in this first attempt.

Get moving on the projects or sections

Personally, I don't work in a wholly organised way. My book writing is much more organic than that and at this stage it's really time to let the big ideas take over. But one caveat; don't expect your final book to be anything like your first over-dramatic ideas. My advice? Reach for the stars and be happy to come back with the moon, which will be pretty impressive in itself, right?

My methods aren't based on anyone else's methods as I have never learned the accepted way of doing things having always been something of a maverick. Sometimes it can be difficult to write and make at the same time. It's a bit like juggling creative skills. If you really enjoy the innovation, you can come up with ideas, write them down, test them and then if they work they are in if they don't work they are out.

Some of you will already have all the projects prepared for classes you have given or online tutorials you have taught. They may be ideas you have tested over and over.

You can share with your friends and family that you are writing but keep a few secrets and surprises from everybody. For now ... just write. You can throw it out and write a better version at the end when the book is ready to go. If you want to go the publisher route, this intro will be useful for your synopsis.

By the way much of your writing will be wholly unedited and in a very raw form. Editing is a different process which comes much later.

> If you worry about crafting each page to perfection before moving on, your creativity will die of boredom.

Be prepared to ditch half of your work. Keep all your finished craft work in a box and make sure you photograph everything you do. No worries about typos, etc. at this stage. Fiddling too much would stifle your flow. Make notes on the side or in the text where you want to include a photograph or illustration. You can revisit this later but If you have the work to hand, do it now, otherwise you have to do the whole thing again. Note: sometimes doing the whole process that you are describing again, to check your instructions, is important though.

Whenever you do share parts of your work with friends/fans/patrons, etc. actively encourage feedback, both positive and negative, and never, never take it personally! You don't necessarily want only "It's absolutely wonderful." Those reviews are nice but not the most helpful. Listen to the "but" after that word. You'll get your most useful information from those "but"s or those "maybe"s. Two types of people will give you harsher criticism. Those who really want you to succeed will give you hard but valuable truths. Listen to them! Then there are those, only a very few, who really want you to fail. Ignore them. You might hear from them again in a negative review or rating. If you don't have your own envious review-sniper, you aren't doing it right!

Where am I going to keep my work and backups?

In the past I always wrote directly into Open Office and had my husband keep backups both on his machine and then on a dedicated backup hard drive. Since working with my daughter on our Your Creative Business book I now write into Google Docs online. This makes Frank blanch, and he insists that I always keep backups of that too. And I agree with him. Well, I have to really. I don't trust tech companies totally to give a bleep about our work, its security or even its safety. But also I can make really dreadful mistakes taking chunks of work to an editing software and then accidentally replacing them incorrectly. So I'd rather be paranoid when it comes to big chunks of my life, like, for example, a hundred days or just over 3 months of my life. Could you easily take a loss of half your income for 3 months? Even a day's loss can be harrowing especially if you lose some of your best work. It's not fun. So take care of your work. Every hour you put in is valuable. If you are using a standard old-fashioned document such as Open Office, save everything you are writing every few lines. If you have just written a detailed explanation of some process and you haven't saved it, your electricity or battery might give in. Control save, or file save, or whatever your program hands you, every few minutes. Google Docs does this for you. The fact that I don't control it does make me anxious especially as my computer has a nasty habit of crashing mid sentence. The most important things to remember to save in Google Docs are your notes in the sidebar. I wondered for ages why, if it was saving every few seconds, it asked me whether I really wanted to close the programme. It turns out I wasn't saving my comments.

> In my book Your Creative Business, I explain how valuable it can be making your work pay more than once by reusing content. Never forget this. Re-using content can make the difference between a profitable business and an unprofitable one.

Save everything in folders that are labelled, so you know where to find everything and the exact path to take. I'm a scatterbrained worker, so this is even more important for me. Frank, who is more methodical, seems to manage without quite so much 'tidying away'.

Your readers' problems are your problems

Be prepared to be really self-critical. That is not to say that you should get yourself a massive dose of artist impostor syndrome. If you've made a design that simply doesn't work for the public or would be difficult for them to achieve good results, be prepared to work on it until it absolutely will work for them. It's no good saying "well if they can't solve those problems that's their fault". If they can't solve problems, you're the teacher so it's probably your fault.

You have to take into account all the most likely mistakes and give leeway for them. For example, I was doing a lobster pot design for a 3D pen for an Etsy pattern. I had to make part of the pattern longer to take into account likely over application of filament. I also had to write up problems caused by under application and how to curve previously applied filament. I'd already drawn this same lobster pot 6 times and had 6 different slight errors which have made me tweak the pattern and the method. This is a material and a method that many of my readers have not come across before. I needed to know that they are going to have some sort of success with it.

Think about it this way. If you present your clever methods in an "of course, you can do this!" way, and the public really can't, you're going to get nothing but bad reviews or no reviews at all; even if your own work is stunningly good.

If your book is intended to teach, then your instructions have to be almost idiot proof. This may mean you tweak away from complicated perfection towards glorious simplicity. These things have not only to look effortless but also to be as low effort as possible. After all, your book is there to entertain. To have fun with. Any obvious mistakes will jar with the reader.

Lastly, if you have a tricky task in a project, and you don't warn your reader in advance that this bit will be difficult, you will make the reader feel small instead of lifting them up. There is no harm in having a difficult bit, but if you let the reader know it will be difficult, they will tackle it as a challenge rather than getting frustrated.

How to use your 100 day planner

My labelled sections on the next 2 pages just give you a vague notion on how long you might spend on each process. The downloadable template is not marked.

Download them from:

www.angiescarr.com/blog

We have designed 2 styles of planner according to how each of us work and we feel its worth including both. I'm very visual and I see 100 days as 3 notional 30 day months and an extra 10 days. Frank however sees 100 days as 14 weeks plus an extra 2 days. You might have a third way of doing it. However you decide to split up your time you need to decide how long you feel you will spend on each task and set an idea of your publication date at the end. We always run overtime whatever date we set but it always helps to have a framework to hang your work on. I'm all for changing your plans whenever they don't quite fit, or if you can do a better job given a few more days or weeks. Or you might even want to spend less time and get your book out sooner. The whole idea of the 100 days is just to give you a little extra discipline if you think it will help you to get your project done.

Nobody is standing behind you with a whip. And that's the point. I, like many creatives, occasionally give in to "can't be bothered" and you might still do that in the middle of 100 days. No worries. Just get back on the horse whenever you're ready. But If you do stick to it you will have a book in 100 days, or not much more. And you'll be able to keep your business going if you choose to write about what you are making ... or make as stock what you are writing about in the book. Because lets face it, very few of us can go 3 months without any income. For that reason we've split every day into AM and PM so that you can choose just to do just an hour, or half a day on the book each day. The very best way of doing this though, is to try to combine production with creation. For example I would write for an hour or so each morning while my brain is "sparking" and then I would do the next making task and photograph for the rest of the day. Then just because of the way I work (making miniatures) I would do any multiples of that day's work in the evening in front of the telly, to build stock.

Would this work for you? It could be a tough 100 days but you can do it and plan a treat or at least a rest after!

100 Day Time Planner

Style 1 - 3x 30 day (months) plus 10 days contingency

	Month 1			Month 2			Month 3	
	am	*pm*		*am*	*pm*		*am*	*pm*
Week 1 - planning			First market research			Editing		
Initial writing and photography			More formal writing and photography (write to market)			Layout (photo editing and formatting)		
						Publishing		

am	*pm*	*am*	*pm*	*am*	*pm*	*am*	*pm*
						10 days contingency	

Style 2 - 14 weeks

Week 1

Week 2

Week 3

Week 4

Week 5

Week 6

Week 7

Week 8

Week 9

Week 10

Week 11

Week 12

Week 13

Week 14

Contingency

Part 3: Photography

"How do people get those nice smart photographs which seem to jump off the page?"

Although we think of ourselves as amateur photographers, our experience is with photographing the production of miniatures step-by-step for publication. When the work you do means that each step will destroy the last, you can't go back and simply do it again, so it's very important to get each step right. The following are our "hacks" for getting professional-looking photographs with an amateur set-up.

Firstly, you need a camera that's up to the job. These days, that may well be your smartphone especially if you're adept at adjusting the brightness settings on your phone camera. If you're buying a smartphone to use as a camera, either for video or stills, look for reviews of the camera capability. We are currently using a smartphone, and having decent results that are certainly good enough for print.

Backgrounds

Our best piece of advice is to photograph against a white background in almost every case. You can change your background colour later if you must. White backgrounds help you to clean up any colour problems in the photo editing software, which can tell the colour balance of the lighting used. We know a number of crafters who shoot their photographs on top of cheap white Ikea coffee tables or white goods such as tumble driers. Anything with a clean, flat, matte pure white surface can do, to start out with!

The most cost-effective and convenient method is to use a white sheet of paper as a backdrop. For small items simply curve it up against the wall of your workspace or booth to create a smooth background. This minimises shadows and provides a clean appearance.

Unless the object is white or has white edges, this background is the simplest and most

Even in our cluttered workspace, diffused light and a simple piece of white paper curved up behind the object makes for a sharp image that can be cut out

The shot cropped and edited for final use. Corner unit SVG design Lisa Sones-Peck

convenient way to make cutouts easily. Frank believes removing the background from the images makes a massive difference, even if it just gives you the opportunity to remove the 'block' shape from the layout. Simply adding the space around images by removing the surplus background makes them 'pop' in print.

If you have to use a coloured background, avoid the gradient commonly used for jewellery. It is not only very much overdone and becoming dated but also restricts the shape of your final image and therefore your artistic options.

Think about the books you really like and look at the way their photographs are presented. Look at what excites the eye and what looks dull. Even if you aren't a designer, thinking in this way will lead you to make the best possible photographs that a designer can work with. If your hands have to be in the shot then you will have defined spaces and defined edges but you might not always need to do so.

Image resolution

Let's keep this simple. We aren't all photographers or mathematicians.

It's very important that you use no less than 150 dpi (dots per inch). You could also talk about pixels and centimetres. It's best you get an idea of what both mean so that photographers or printing departments don't bamboozle you. Simply put, and rounded up a bit, if you have an image which is 100 pixels wide, it's not going to look really sharp if it's printed more than a centimetre wide. The better your resolution, the larger you can print your image without it looking grainy or pixelated. The higher quality you can get, the better. You should ideally never go below 150 DPI in the finished print as it would look blurred.

We currently use a midrange Samsung phone with 48 megapixels (a megapixel is 1,000 x 1,000 dots). Bear in mind that there's nothing wrong with buying second-hand equipment, including cameras and phones, just ensure that the lens isn't scratched before you buy.

Make or buy a tripod or stand to hold your camera. Ours is a cheap makeshift piece of equipment held together with wood and elastic bands. But you don't see that from the photos, so who cares?

150 DPI image

10 DPI image

Lighting

The most important part of photography is lighting. If there is too much light you may lose details because of a bleaching out effect. If there is too little light, images can be grainy. Don't take pictures in full sun as it has to be diffused to avoid heavy shadows. We found direct sunlight quite unhelpful for photography, especially as it changes direction and colour through the day. Having said that you can play with shadows as an artistic decision.

We are lucky enough to have an internal white walled glass roofed patio. This provides endless diffused sunlight most days. Our normal work is 12th scale miniatures. It can be tricky to get light to the miniature if you have the lens right against it for Macro mode. Our preference is never to use Macro mode as it often blurs half the image in a stylised way. On phones Macro mode may also have fewer megapixels. We normally use a high megapixel camera in standard mode. This leaves a modestly sized image in the centre of a larger area. If you start at 48 megapixels you can crop it down to just 12 and still have a very useable image for a full page of a book.

The original shot in a small, folding, LED lighting box

Cropped and edited

You won't always be able to photograph in diffused daylight. For very small work you can buy very reasonably priced small LED lightboxes, or LED ring lights which have become very popular for vloggers and make up artists for lighting faces evenly - I also use mine for live classes in my workshop. These can also be used as overhead lights and can function as a tripod for your camera even when you're not using the light. Do bear in mind that some ring lights are designed to only hold a phone, and some are only designed to hold a standard camera, although some do both. Another option is to go to a photography shop, if you have any disposable capital and buy a photographer's light tent. We've never invested money in those but so far, we haven't needed to. The smaller ones are OK for very small items, but you may need a larger area to put your hands into.

You don't need an expensive set up for this either.

You can build a light box using cheap pre-stretched large rectangular canvases. Screw together making a box with five sides and an open front. You can use strips of full spectrum LEDs in the box. All these components are available in the large import shops, the lights can even be Xmas lights. One warning: both ring and strip lights can leave nasty reflections on your work so be very aware of the angles you take your photographs from.

For even larger work you could use white bed sheets to create a "booth".

With your item positioned against the white backdrop, touch the screen of your smartphone until you have a nice sharp focus. If it won't focus close up, you will have to take the picture from a little further away.

Before you take a photograph look at the screen and check you aren't shadowing any part of the object. Then move the camera around until it fills as much of the screen as possible without causing other issues. Tip the camera up or down to change the viewpoint, and move around from left to right. We normally take photos at various angles and choose on the computer what looks best. It costs nothing, and leaves you with choices later.

Process shots (step-by-steps)

One little trick we do when photographing hands in the process of working is to set the timer to about 5 seconds then place a business card or calling card (ideally with small writing) at the depth where the hands will be. This often simply means putting it on the side of one hand if you are working and photographing alone. We click to focus on the card, and then remove the card, placing the hands back in shot in time for the shutter click. It usually works. This is also good for ultra-close ups where there are still things at several depths. The business card will set the highest of the focus depths and anything behind will still look good. If you try to focus on a deeper part, you can lose the closer parts.

For close work you can also buy neck mounted camera phone holders very cheaply. Get one with a swivelling mount so you can take both portrait and landscape shots. When doing very small work it can be difficult to see what you are doing through or round the camera so you might need to practise with a set up like this.

So now you have the best, sharpest image possible to work with, and you can then use all the tools on your photo editing software to make it even better. This is pretty simple if your background is clean and white because any colour balance issues will be easily rectified.

If photographing larger items, such as clothing or large artworks, you may need to back your lighting off a long way. Have as many sources as possible from as many different directions and remember to light your model from underneath as well as above. Shadows from overhead lighting may be moody but are unlikely to make your work or your model look their best. There may be times to use unusual lighting, such as at Halloween, however, your goal is usually to just have a sharp and well-lit image, without harsh shadows.

Whatever size you're working with, remember the spectrum of the light you're working with will affect your basic picture, but you can usually tweak that later in Photoshop, Krita, or whatever photo editing software you're using. The key is to get enough light and good focus.

One thing is for certain. If you get a really good image, under really good diffused light and on a white background, anyone who knows anything about images (for example a magazine's art department) will know what to do to present your work at its very best. If you're completely stuck, there are people on websites like Fiverr who can edit a batch for you for around "a fiver" each, more or less.

When you have your first lovely pictures, keep your very best in a file you call something like "best images", so you know where to go for all your most beautiful shots. If you can learn the photo editing skills, get into the habit of making compilations of these for book promotions.

Photo editing and image optimisation appears later in this book as it's best done in a batch when you are making artistic decisions.

Takeaway

Good images are crucial to the look of your book, so it's well worth your while investing time or even money in learning more. With practice, you can certainly get good quality images from a good smartphone these days. Think light, light and more light and try to photograph on a white background. The rest can be done afterwards, by someone else if necessary.

Part 4: Carrying on writing

(The ups and downs of the creative muse)

One way to trigger the muse is to write always ... or just whenever you are moved to do so. The other way is to read, read, read.

Why do we often feel we have to perform like some kind of superhuman? Sometimes we really do just need time off to recharge. Impostor syndrome is real, of course but I like to think "writer's block" is just the natural biorhythmic ups and downs of your creative muse. Maybe you're just tired!

I'm sure everyone who is on this journey has already had a "what am I doing" moment, when the task looks too big. If you haven't ... you will.

Although I think we should find at least an hour in every one of these days when we do some written work towards the book. Real life means that we, who work from home don't always have a time blocked out for work in the office, and we really need to act as if we do sometimes.

Falling off the writing wagon isn't the end of the world. I've stopped writing several times in the middle of books because something got in the way. Either I just wasn't feeling it, or another project was more tempting. Those books got written anyway. This very book is one that I started over two years ago. I've realised several times in my life that even though I try, there is just one thing that I can't do, no matter how motivated ... and that is everything! So the other way to be a writer or any kind of creator is to ride the creative waves. That means, that like a surfer, you may spend some time just paddling round in slack water until that wave comes. See whether your muse wants you to take things slowly. Be mildly creative or write your heart out.

These days instead of fighting the ups and downs of the creative muse, I've found the waves actually help me, if I work with them rather than against. Of course it's easier when you're approaching retirement and already have a dozen or more books behind you but I do think that the modern 9-5 mentality leads to lifetimes of potential wasted in guilt trips and forcing out poor quality work when you really can't bring out your best inspiration.

I don't want to make it too easy on you though. So if you want a prompting task, here it is. If you haven't already found more advanced text editing tools check them out. I wrote nearly all my books without an editor ... and unfortunately, it shows. My run-on sentences can make my writing difficult to read and it's only now that I'm fully aware of it. It was only a few years ago when I had already published half my books, that I even knew such programs existed. I started to look at my work with just a little more care. So, here are two to try.
www.scribens.com
prowritingaid.com
Ignore their offers of a sample text and paste your work directly in. They are not perfect and have a habit of giving false information about text spacing. Layout software needs two spaces after a full stop. Even I find myself blindly accepting their decision to put only one.

How best to start your writer's day

Personally I don't start by getting up and then just expecting myself to write. I start by reading in bed. Sometimes I'm already buzzing with ideas, and I quickly put my Kindle down and jump out of bed so I can get started as quickly as possible. Sometimes I have a slow "lazy" get up and am reading for an hour. Sometimes jotting down notes of ideas that my reading has triggered.

Often they can be books unrelated to the book I'm working on. Reading the words of an accomplished writer can almost turn your mind into that of an eloquent accomplished writer too. It can switch your creativity on.

So here is my faking it until you make it trick. Remember if you are creative you are anything you want to be. If you want to be a writer today, you need to open up to a writer's mindset. If you want to be a performer, you need to take a deep breath. Drop your shoulders and let out your inner great performer.

Imagination exercise

You have to imagine yourself in the role of a successful artist or writer before you can be one. Just as an actor has to think himself into the part he's playing. It's not inauthentic. It is, in fact, the actor allowing himself to be totally authentic in that role.

So reading other people's words and having them trigger your own is channelling rather than any kind of plagiarism. This morning for example I was reading "You're Not Listening" by Kate Murphy. Nothing to do with writing craft books? Well actually it is. If you don't listen to your readers' fears and problems you aren't going to be able to solve them.

This is a good trick whatever art you are undertaking. It's allowing your mind to open up and let inspiration flow, rather than imagining yourself as unsuccessful, which stifles your creativity.

I've hinted at the inner demons that might stop you writing, especially the artist's impostor syndrome. Maybe we don't resolve that inner conflict by swatting at and belittling ourselves. What we really need to do with our inner demons is to confront them with reason. They are powerless against that. If you want to know more about the "is it really true?" reasoning, look at "The Work of Byron Katie".

The dynamics of your book

Let's dig a little deeper into style. A long time ago a very good and smart friend of mine, Dave Whatt, who was teaching me guitar, told me a rule I should stick by and I did ... and it worked. "When playing for an audience" he said, "play loud and quiet, fast and slow, high ... and low". I won't go into the full story of how I learned this to be true as that's part of another book. Sufficient to say that you don't need to be full on upbeat throughout the whole book. There is time for quiet contemplation, time for big doses of inspiration. Time for humour. So your book needs to be punctuated with beautiful images of finished work and part made work and needs to have step-by-steps regularly. If it's all step-by-step it will be informative but there is no interaction with the author. If there is no flow there is no beauty and no artistic dynamic to keep people interested. You want your book to be one of the most interesting on the market even if it's not perfect. Again, remember who you are, who your reader is and what they want.

Like my guitar playing back in the day. I was not anywhere near as good as my peers. But since I learned that rule about dynamics, at least my performance was interesting.

Writing exercise

For a more interesting tone, try writing one paragraph as if you were chatting to a friend on the sofa, showing your work. Then write the same paragraph being a little silly. Maybe making fun of yourself. Now write something as if you were a lecturer in a big hall doing a TED talk show-and-tell presentation with a big screen behind you.

So you have three styles there: humble and gracious, humorous and authoritative. You can choose to use one, or all those sides of yourself in your presentation of your book.

Maybe your introduction could be funny. The main body of the project needs to get the information across and be easy to understand and the round up could be humble. Or you could swap 1 and 3 around. Start out gently presenting the idea. Show it clearly and then, if you want to be the friendly mentor, drop in anecdotes about the many ways it can all go terribly wrong thus allowing for failure and making the reader much more relaxed about having a go themselves.

All this may not come naturally to you. You may naturally be one or the other of those personalities: humble, authoritative, funny or relaxed. But I do believe that getting the dynamics into your work can be as easy as thinking yourself into the role. Use your own words and your own style but have another something up your sleeve to colour some parts a slightly different colour, or 'mood' if you like.

Craft authors generally want people to buy their physical book. You want them to buy it because they are able to dip in and out of the projects (if you're putting projects in) but you also want ebook buyers to read the ebook cover to cover because that's another place where you can make money. If you are producing an ebook, the pages aren't as attractive so your book needs to have an interesting "flow". Incidentally ebook buyers will often buy the paperback too.

You don't need your reader to know why they keep coming back to your books. You just need them to find your books more engaging than most. If they do, they will become your super readers and it will usually be down to a sort of literary and artistic "texture".

How do you choose to put your project together?

I have a couple of friends who write using a voice recorder with a text writing option. Both of them have their best ideas when doing mundane tasks. Most creative people report a surge of inspiration first thing in the morning so maybe grabbing the voice recorder will help. We can pooh-pooh new tech as not "writing" but what really matters? The finished book, right? Whether you favour pencil and paper by the bed or taking your laptop everywhere, or you prefer a set hour to sit yourself in front of that blank screen, they all add up to the same thing. Recording your thoughts before they escape. But here's the thing. The paper, the screen or the recorder are all blank before you fill them and what if the ideas just aren't coming. Is there a trick to force them out? No there really isn't, except to say that you have to keep exercising even if you don't want to go to the gym. So you have to keep at the job even if you don't come out with pearls every day.

This isn't a novel we're writing here (unless it is). All we have to do is get our craft inspiration down as step-by-step projects or show-and-tell advice for other aspiring creatives.

But here's a little secret. Sometimes I don't feel like making the article first and then writing up how I did it. Sometimes I do it the other way round. I make a guess at how I might do it, write that up briefly, and then go and check my theory by doing the make.

This isn't always how I do it but it is my basic method for new ideas and it means I'm doing the writing at the best time. When I'm still excited by the project and noticing every process and not bored enough to imagine it's easy. Because that's what we do when we've done something ten times. We forget the sticking points. That is unhelpful to the beginner.

How self-disciplined are you? Another secret. I'm not! Not at all. I procrastinate about procrastinating. I'll do almost anything to avoid getting down to it. So self-discipline is just this. Saying to yourself It's only a very small bite you have to do and when you've done that you can have a coffee. What often happens is when you get started you find the inspiration flowing. You just have to get over that hurdle of feeling uninspired just this minute.

How quickly will you hit the wall? Maybe you already have. You will hit it several times through the project. The days when you say "I'm not a writer. Everyone is better than me." That's the impostor syndrome. And everyone goes through it; except narcissists. But that's the great thing about having a target deadline. Sometimes real life does step in... or health problems. But if you forgive yourself for your trips and move on as soon as you can you will still be going in the right direction. The only people who won't have a book of some kind at the end of this are those that simply give up (physical and mental health issues and family crises apart, of course).

Take baby steps at first and then there will be days when you will get a chunk done just because you enjoyed some success. If you are doing this as a 100 day challenge make sure you do something every day. Set yourself a very small goal and if it doesn't work out, we'll call that a practice run.

So if you are still just thinking about it, and you haven't started writing yet, today is the day to start. Write a page. Just one page. Or even just a list of the items needed for a project. Or an outline about how a tool works.

What to do with procrastination

Procrastination can be useful if you always have alternative tasks at hand that are equally important.

First try not procrastinating. Go to your book and identify a task that is reasonably easy and achievable. Perhaps writing one page about tools. One morning in the middle of one book I remembered that there was one type of spatula that was best to use when stencilling so I wrote about it for the Patreon page first. Of course I knew that idea would be re-used when I needed to write about stencilling again. When you use one piece of work for more than one purpose you are effectively finding a way to pay yourself twice for the same work. That really matters when you are writing, because there's precious little income coming in at those times. So I share early details and hints with my patrons and in return they help keep the wolf from the door during the "hungry" writing phase.

"I haven't got time"

My inner demon is often "I haven't got time". I told myself this most of this weekend and then proceeded to spend a lot of that time on the internet. Any creative work can't be considered a waste of time and will be very valuable in the future. Don't let it become "I've got no time" procrastination, though. This is a symptom of overwhelm. The best thing you can do is to catch it early and deal with it.

Life does often get in the way and the stresses of everyday life and families can often scupper the best laid plans. One extra perceived pressure on top of another can bring the whole lot tumbling down.

What can you do?

The thing I always go back to is the "get a plan, change a plan, get another plan", mantra. You aren't as stuck as you think.

Try going back to using a personal organiser.

Go back to that idea of eating the elephant bite by bite. If you haven't heard that one look it up. A personal information manager can really help you to focus on chopping up your day into time slots and then assigning time and priority to tasks. I know it might all feel a bit formulaic and against your arty anarchistic tendencies (those of us who are arty and anarchistic) but what you have to remember is that you are in charge and can change the plan at any time. It's not, "nobody tells me what to do" it's more the obvious second half of the sentence " - but me!"

> Plan which parts of your book you are going to squeeze into next week. Start by having a meeting with yourself or anyone you work with on a Monday morning.

How much time have you got? How much do you think you can achieve in that time? Make sure there's some fun in there and it's not all slog. Which are the pages you most want to write? Or do you want to make and photograph first? Then try your best to stick to that but forgive yourself if your muse takes you off in a different direction. Just so long as you get back to the plan or tweak the plan to fit your new ideas as quickly as possible. You don't have to write the beginning before the end. You are the boss. And you can have pudding before dinner if you want!

Remember to make those goals achievable because there's no feeling like making or even surpassing a goal!

Refining your style

So you've started writing. You've got a bit of an outline and an introduction and even made and written up some projects. But you don't really have a serious idea what your book will look like or how you're going to make it flow.

This is a good time to remind you to keep going back to your audience/reader. Remind yourself who your audience are and how you want to reach out to them. This first week or two is mostly about thinking about your book and your writing. You have probably started writing but you certainly don't want to be too hard on yourself if you still feel confused and disorganised. Right now you might have very little idea exactly where you are jumping off from, let alone where you're going.

Do you remember the initial planning chapter? At this stage one trick is not to look at how you want to write. Look at how you **don't** want to write. Don't think about how you want your book to look. Think only about how you **don't** want it to look.

What annoys you about certain books? What do you think you could do better? What are your pet peeves?

Maybe you don't like books that are just like text books with too many words. Not enough images?

Maybe you don't like how to books that have loads of images and very little text and you want to produce something "meaty".

You could decide that you want to produce a coffee table book that is all beautiful images of your perfect work and no instructions at all. That actually could be great too. I have in mind a couple of artists for whom that would definitely be the way forward. Ones who keep their secrets and whose work is to be admired and envied, and who have a real way with presentation. But that's not me. It's a perfectly valid format for a coffee table book which would appeal more to collectors than makers, although there would be a crossover. There could be makers who would buy with the intent to copy your wonderful work. Or just because your images are so stunning and unattainable.

> So what do you not like, and what would you write/create instead?

Personally I don't like "writers who write as they think writers ought to write". Neither do I enjoy being taught by teachers who set themselves up as the unattainable perfection. That is to say pompous overblown dictatorial "I'm better than you" writing. Words and images that say "My work is better than yours will ever be, but this is what you could hope to achieve if you do it as long as I have". So as the opposite of what I don't like, I hope my writing says "This is just an idea of what you might like to do. Here are a few tips about what to try. Here are the mistakes I've made and here are some sure-fire successes."

There is a drawback to all of this. Your readers will produce better work than you. You're a writer and teacher now and you can see that as a mark of your success! If you don't want people to copy you, this is the time to stop thinking about writing a book, it won't make you happy. If you can be happy being the wind under other creatives' wings, this is for you. Your book will be popular, but your work will be superseded. If you still want to write your book, you have only one option. Accept that your work will be copied and that your readers will produce stunningly beautiful work that makes yours look like a beginner. Content yourself that you are putting people on that road to success. They may never even acknowledge your existence when they are bathed in the kudos of their own achievement. But you'll know! And hopefully you'll have a bestseller, or at least a book that some people will really cherish. When someone does thank you for lifting them up, it's a feeling like no other.

So when you've thought about these knotty problems and you still want to write and you know what book you don't want to produce - write down a mission statement for yourself. Start "I want to write a book that ...". You can add several "ands".

Here's mine: "I want to write a book that helps other creatives to self-publish their own craft and DIY tutorial books ... and that makes them believe in themselves as potential authors ... and that helps them add to their income streams".

Market research prior to marketing is a long old job but it may also help you to title and prepare your book for the market as well as preparing you to market your book. So if you really can't make yourself write today, try looking at marketing.

Part 5: Marketing strategy

Researching and planning

It's never too early to think about marketing.

When it looks like this book is really going to happen, it's time to prepare the ground for a more fruitful marketing campaign later.

Social media

You've already thought about your ideal customer. Where do they hang out? Which Facebook groups are they in? Do they use Pinterest or Instagram? Are you using all those media? Do you post helpful comments under other people's posts? Do you appreciate and comment on their work or their efforts, even when the work is beginner level? Are you supportive or competitive? There are authors who are clearly more competitive than supportive and you can see that in their posts.

Of course it's going to be the case that your book will be the solution for a lot of people but only if you listen. If you have an answer, give it generously and without strings and keep that carefully crafted answer in your book folder in case it comes in handy later. Don't pooh-pooh anyone else's answers and do lift up your friends who have got there before you in the conversation. Lift up other authors. Book buyers don't only buy one book on a subject. Good karma really does come around and very quickly in the crafts business and bad karma, though rare in this business … is bad. So start building an audience right now, but build it through your generosity not by your competitiveness.

Do a bit of friendly checking in to your groups. Is there a type of group related to the subject of your book that doesn't exist yet that you could open up? For our "Your Creative Business book" which is a companion to this one now, there really weren't many truly supportive groups for all small creative businesses so I started the Your Creative Business Facebook group. It goes a lot further than the subjects of my books. Of course it's related and so it's a good place to direct the sort of people who will really get something from that book and although it takes some time to admin' it's also a great place to share my problems and find out about other people's needs. It brings together other people who might help each other. The idea is to make it work for my book but also work for the members between them. Can you do something like that in advance of your book coming out? Giving support to others on a subject related to your book helps build your authority in that field. One caution. Don't talk about what you don't know about. It makes you look foolish. That would be anti-marketing. Let someone else take the lead.

It may be that Twitter is the better place to hang out if the people who are interested in your subject are there. You aren't constrained by group admins and can keep looking in on the hashtags that interest you and that are relevant to your reader group. For example, if you are writing a sustainable DIY book you may find gathering follows from others interested in green issues is a good idea. And this can take a long time; so do start now.

Never forget, no matter how old you are, the power of short videos including TikTok, Instagram and Pinterest. Put some of your most gorgeous images out there and ask questions and give answers.

Do not get into the habit of asking irrelevant questions. This is an awful social media fad which is getting annoying. But it is true that relevant questions garner relevant responses from relevant people! These people could become your important first buyers and your supportive friends.

Some market research into comparable books

If you haven't started looking at the comparable book market, here is a market research and marketing task that will help you be ready when the time comes to publish and may well help you with some of your decisions about where to place your book in the market.

Go and look on Amazon for similar titles and themes to the book you are writing. Write them all down. Next to them write either the ISBN number or the ASIN (Amazon Standard Identification Numbers on ebooks). Look at the categories that the books have been placed in. In some cases these will not be what you expect but generally craft books will come under a fairly tight set of categories.

Here is a breakdown from Amazon of my **Making Miniature Food and Market Stalls** book. This was not self-published and although the sales figures are lower than my current book the numbers are still pretty good. Although they have been better. The best seller rank is current and not historical, so do be aware your rankings can fall as well as rise.

Product details
Item Weight : 1.3 pounds / 590g
Paperback : 144 pages
ISBN-13 : 978-1784944445
Dimensions : 8.3 x 0.5 x 10.8 inches
Publisher : GMC Publications; Updated edition (August 7, 2018)
Language : English
Best Sellers Rank: #374,578 in Books (See Top 100 in Books)
#55 in Polymer Clay
#90 in Miniatures
Customer Reviews: 4.8 out of 5 stars 181 ratings

Look at the best sellers rankings

You are looking at successful books to align yourself to, and you are looking for the categories under which they are placed. You need to know the best categories to be in when you publish to Amazon.

Its also interesting to see their size, weight and dimensions to see if your book will fit on the bookshelf of your target customer alongside other comparable books.

Compare this with our recent miniatures book **The Dollhouse Flower Shop**.

Product details
Item Weight : 6.6 ounces / 188g
Paperback : 52 pages
ISBN-13 : 978-1687037923
Dimensions : 8.27 x 0.13 x 10.98 inches
Publisher : Independently published (August 21, 2019)
Language : English
Best Sellers Rank: #191,744 in Books (See Top 100 in Books)
#17 in Dollhouses (Books)
#34 in Miniatures
#38 in Stenciling
Customer Reviews: 4.6 out of 5 stars 46 ratings

You will see that at the time of looking even though the first book has sold 40 thousand copies plus, and this one just a few hundred so far, it is currently more popular than the first one, at this time it was pretty good at 17 in Dollhouses. It's briefly been at number one in some markets too.

Now for those of you who are really competitive, let me tell you what keeping your book secret from your competition does for you. Well, precisely nothing. Whereas aligning yourself with your competitors is a great thing to do. Being a competitor is not a bad thing; it's a great thing. Just like having a wedding gown shop on a road that's full of wedding gown shops is far from a bad thing. That road is going to attract more brides-to-be and they are going to pass your shop too. Unlike wedding gown shops though, crafts people rarely buy only one book. They will buy all of your books as well as the comparable ones. So don't hide your light. Importantly, don't refuse to connect for fear that a customer may choose another person's book over yours. A few may, but it's more likely that they will see all of your books almost as a series, and will buy the lot. If you are disconnected, someone may find your book by accident ... but it's too rare.

All this research has another use, and this is why you keep those ISBNS and ASINS. This is to help you if you want to look back to check how books are doing, but it also helps you if and when you decide to give your book a push on Amazon advertising.

Look at other information in these listings too. When was the book published? How many ratings have they got? Read the bad reviews and resolve to address any real issues that need to be better in your book. What did the customers love? Be aware that some reviews are from friends so cut through the sycophancy to the real information.

For pricing later you might be interested in their format and number of pages. However be aware that some books are overpriced and some cheap in more ways than one. Don't join a race to the bottom.

Think about co-operating

When comparing your book to someone else's: if you find another author who has written a book in the same genre as yours but covers a different topic, try reaching out to them. They may be co-operative rather than competitive. Perhaps you can share eager customers who are going to want their book as well as yours and vice versa, thus doubling both of your sales ... win win! Not everybody is reciprocal and co-operative but its well worth being open to collaborative marketing efforts. My experience is that collaborations work.

Secrecy ... and openness

Your final title must be secret, but other bits can be released.

Get a provisional title and a working title. Use only your working title even when talking to friends.

Keep the title you think you will use in the end secret (monkey hear monkey do). You don't want to be competing with someone else using your title because they've heard it somewhere and think it was in their head. Use a working title.

You may need to keep other little secrets just to make sure your work isn't copied in its entirety but what makes a craft/creative book popular is when you do give away secrets that people have been wondering about. If you're an author, you need to be as open as possible.

Personally I believe you can release your theme once you are fairly certain that you are actually going to get this book finished in reasonably short order. It takes a while to write a book (as you know) and if you are going to take 3 months (as we are) you can be pretty confident that once you are a month or so in, nobody is going to overtake you. If they do, then they will have either rushed it and have a pretty poor result, or put a lot of work into the subject themselves and probably deserve their success. You can also be pretty happy that your book, having taken a little longer, will sit well alongside another with a similar theme.

Pictures. You can release low resolution versions of your book photos at any time ... and you should. Save some work for later, but don't be afraid to show off your best work. It will whet your customers' appetites.

Marketing hint

Start keeping names of people who have shown interest in buying your book and ask them if you can add them to your mailing list (pre-marketing).

Individual projects. You might imagine that releasing your projects would be an absolute no-no. But here's why I think you'd be wrong. You need to whip up some real excitement and a desire to read the rest, and there's nothing quite as good as a taster for whetting the appetite. If you don't believe me, several of the projects in my first book were actually released in Dolls House and Miniature Scene Magazine over the two years before that book came out. I could have written separate projects but imagine, if you bought a music album from someone based on their single only to find, that single wasn't in the album? People don't mind seeing things twice as long as they come in a beautiful book that they can keep on their shelves. (This is why people who buy an ebook will often also buy the physical copy as well.) So don't be afraid to say 'This is from my upcoming book on the subject of ... (general theme) and "If you are interested in being kept informed please join my mailing list on… ". Or you can use some other way to contact you. Most authors will attest that mailing lists are the very best way to get early sales. And early sales are the most important of all, as are early reviews. Even if your book is excellent, very few will take the chance to buy if there are no reviews.

Do consider during your writing process offering a magazine early releases of your tutorials. It can be a really fantastic way to kickstart visibility and build an audience for your book.

My first book was written at the same time as my Challenge Angie series in Dolls House and Miniature Scene magazine, and many of the projects in the book are the same as, or similar to those in the magazine. My articles were unusual at the time. Chatty and inspirational. They built a following in that magazine and this was a great step off to make sure the book sales were high on publication. Be sure to let them know that your content will be reproduced in your book but not in any other magazine. Watch out for some magazines which re-publish your work in other magazines in other countries without permission. This can be very embarrassing especially if you have a relationship with a different magazine in the second country. This has happened to me. Write your terms very carefully.

Marketing and positioning problem - artist envy

While you are working your way through these comparable books I have a word of warning; don't get envious of people who are selling a lot of books. Just ask yourself why that is and copy those methods (not those books though!) Nobody's book will be better than yours for your ideal customer.

I want to talk about artist envy because that is one of the things that can hit us pretty shortly after we've started writing. We look at what other people do and start comparing, start envying the successes other people have. We start worrying that our work is not good enough. It happens to me too. A couple of my patrons have said "wouldn't [your work] be better if you did it this way? " and maybe it would! My little worry monster says "Is this really good enough and shouldn't you be proving what an artist you are? " I have to pull myself back together and remember, like I did this morning, what my book is about. Who it's aimed at. I can let my flights of fancy manifest themselves in my own work or play and not necessarily in my tutorial book.

A friend of mine once said of another artist who had taught the whole world to make the most wonderful mini bread "She's overrated". I was annoyed for the other artist. I replied we all look overrated when someone we teach goes on to make even more wonderful work. I told her we really should rate the teacher for being really good at her job. My friend had also forgotten that the work in the artist's tutorials is not representative of her perfectionism in her own work. Some of the artist's students were, of course, going to produce more carefully produced work than that which appeared in her books.

This same friend, who died recently said regretfully, in her final weeks, "I wish I had written a book". Therein lies the injustice of life.

Really, she wanted to imagine that she could both improve on the work of the authors she had learned from, and write the book. It's really not the same thing. A craft author teaches. That's their first job. Their own most carefully considered and executed work may not be in their books and tutorials.

Another polymer clay artist writes books which are very simple and accessible and people could say from looking at them that she is not an artist ... but she really is. She is just doing what is called "writing to market" and she does that very well.

That sounds all very negative, so here's the upside. I have had a good handful of comments from artists I really admire, saying that my books gave them their first inspiration. A good few more who say my books have been their therapy. There is no better feeling than that!

Of course I'm hit with artist envy when someone I've taught goes on to make a better job of the easy work I've taught. But that's one of those undermining demons I have to stomp on.

Take a deep breath when you know you could do a better or more complicated job and ask yourself whether that would serve the purpose of encouraging others to have a go themselves, or not. First ask yourself whether you need to be the best artist or you need to be the best teacher. The people who put out the "For Dummies" series of books are not dummies themselves. They are very successful authors and they do a very good job of making the apparently difficult, accessible; step-by-step.

So let's see if we can do that. Make a book that jumps off the shelves (or the computer screen) and into people's shopping baskets because they can immediately see what you are getting at, and they just know after doing your easy one they are going to personalise the hell out of it! Result! A book sale for you and the warm fuzzy feeling that you might have been the first inspiration for some future great artist.

After that diversion back to market research. You are also looking for books which have lots of good reviews because getting reviews for your books is going to be important to you. You want the same customers who are going to review your books. I really haven't done enough work in this area but am resolved to do more in the future. It's very difficult to get as many reviews as you'd like anyway unless you resort to pay-per-review which I simply won't do. Also, there are some other tricks people use which aren't quite as over-principled as I am. Nevertheless, I'm really happy that the genuine reviews are pretty good! Oh and one early word about reviewers. You have never really made it until you have your own troll reviewer. Don't worry too much about them. They have to have bought a book. If their review is really bad and unfair, they aren't clever enough to realise that one really nasty scathing review among 50 good ones isn't going to mean anything. It tells the reader more about their agenda than it does about your book. If anything it proves that there's something here to be envious of. So, when you have published, let's share troll stories!

Get your customers ready for publication day.

Don't promise free books. Start now getting your friends used to the idea of actually buying your book. If you've already suggested to someone that you might give them a free book its time for the "would you mind...?" discussion.

Your early sales will show Amazon that your book is worth pushing. So, even before you consider putting a penny into advertising, think about what a good idea it is to use that first burst of excitement from your friends to be absolutely the most effective and cheapest advertising you will ever do.

The main thing is to launch with a bang. This is "do as I say, not as I do". Make sure that you get your friends to buy through Amazon. So don't make a big author order. This is the best and cheapest way to get ranked. You may think that you'll make more money from an author order, and you will, in the short term. Then you would put all that money back into advertising which you didn't need to do if only you had directed people to Amazon in the first place. Why is that? Rankings.

Tell your friends you are sorry, but your book-mentor (me) has told you that you absolutely mustn't give any away to friends. That you really need them to buy and you need them to review. Give them anything else. Take them out for a meal or a drink. Send them a box of chocs but don't give them a book.

You can of course tell them why buying a copy is so important to you and that it's worth 10x more than the money.

Your friends may want a signed copy, but more than that they want to see you succeed and being really businesslike about getting actual sales is the first step.

And this is also a really good excuse not to skint yourself trying to be nice to people who won't necessarily even appreciate it. Real friends will absolutely listen to you and completely understand when you explain it to them.

What happens then is that Amazon sees that your book is popular. It also collects the info about the type of buyers; anyone who won't buy your book in spite of you asking nicely, is not a book buyer, so information on them is irrelevant to the buyer profile.

Amazon then creates what's called "look-alike" buyer profiles. They will find people who buy books like yours based on your first customers, and they will push your book at those customers. So, since most of a creative person's friends are other creatives, they find other people like your friends to advertise to. You might notice that Amazon sometimes advertises books to you that are similar to the profile of books you might be writing. Clever eh? But it's because people like you, buy books like that. They know way too much about you don't they?

Because my book is published by Frank, they don't realise that I'm the author, so I get an accidental privileged insight into what Amazon are up to. Because I have bought my books, they think I'm an Angie Scarr book buyer. They also advertise comparable books to me. This is all really useful information because I see when they are pushing my books. And I notice it in the sales figures. For example they were advertising one of my books to me a few days ago and that reflected pretty quickly in my sales figures. Today they showed me another miniaturist's book. I'm not disappointed because I know they will be showing my book to other people. And in any case mine will probably appear in the "People who bought this book also bought..." section, under theirs. They know that people buy craft books for Xmas, I typically double my monthly sales figures during those months and I know why. Amazon is advertising them for free because they know that it works. They know they will make money from those sales and so I get to benefit too.

This is why those first sales are so very important to you, especially from a new author. They show that your book is popular and who it's popular with. That gives them something to work with and hopefully gets those important first reviews too. Every friend you give a book to is depriving yourself of at least 10X that number in onward sales and its cumulative!

Definitely don't give books away. If you really want to give them a gift why not send them a handmade bookmark instead. Every logged sale is worth much more than any kind of author offer.

Your friends can make you famous! I can't stress that enough. Yes, you will need to be courageous asking. And I know especially Brits don't like asking but ASK. Successful people ASK!

For those friends you really wanted to give a copy to; you can give a signed copy, a month down the line. They can pass the first one on to a friend and show off what their friend/relative has done. But first ask them to review your book, because good reviews do tip the balance into a sale. Even moderate reviews are worth having, and only buyers can review.

There is one more thing you can do … if you absolutely must. Especially if you offer a Kindle version, but you can do it for physical copies too. You can send potential reviewers who you know are short of money the cost of your book upfront so they can buy it and be verified buyers. (Doing it in retrospect is, quite rightly, frowned-upon.) I tend to hold this back for the second push if I need it and in fact have only done it with one of my books The Frugalist. Because most people who could use it really are short of money. In any case a good review is definitely worth the cost of one of your books!

Part 6: Preparing your work for publishing

Are you ready to start editing?

As you start to gather your book together from the diverse ideas you start to put them in order. Sometimes that order gets changed to improve the flow of the information. I like to have all my work printed out rather than keeping it all on my computer. One trick I do to see if there really is a flow is to place the sheets on my tiled floor one sheet per tile. Then I walk

all over them to see if each project really does follow naturally from the last. I know it's a lot of paper but you can then gather it back up, sit it on your knee and read through it and see how things really flow in book format. At least 50% of your books will be bought as paperbacks rather than as ebooks so it has to flow as a book. If I still feel as if I'm a bit behind where I'd like to be that's OK. I'm happy then that I can put the right extra bits in the right places.

You might have quite another, less physical and more formal way of checking the flow. I can only tell you how we do it. I do enjoy the "floor day" because it's the first time that my random projects really do start to look like a publishable body of work. Of course our two cats love to get involved too. It doesn't always help.

If you haven't already joined ALLi (The ALLiance of independent authors) this is a very good time to do it. However I'm sorry to say it's not cheap for the struggling creative. Their info will help you avoid a lot of heartache especially when buying in help.

Do you need an editor? Can you afford one? If you can afford an editor you absolutely should. I have never been able to afford a professional editor, and I would admit, it shows. Especially in my earlier self-published books.

If like me you can't, I think the best thing might be to pair up with someone else who is writing at the same time, maybe in a different genre so your work doesn't influence each other too much. You are then able to critique each other's work, hopefully without oversensitivity. You have to drop any ego to listen to critique though, which isn't always comfortable. But someone who tells you exactly what you want to hear is no use to you.

Even if you can afford an editor, It's going to save you a lot of money if you can do your own grammar checking and pre-editing to a second draft. I now use a free programme Scribens. I definitely wouldn't say it was the best on the market but it does help and it is free. This is another place AI can help you. I've recently used ChatGPT when I got stuck on a phrase that just didn't seem to flow well or make much sense.

You can also ask AI to check for common mistakes or to help you rewrite sentences and meanings you are grappling unsuccessfully with. I feel sure these uses and many more are going to be one of the self-published author's best friends. It might also cause us many headaches as it will be, and I believe is being, used to produce substandard work in its entirety. Those books will appear on the same platform as our work. Don't rely on it too heavily because there could be questions about who owns the copyright of what could be considered semi-plagiarised work, given that it has learned everything from other authors.

Check any self-editing again, again and again, but do at least get comments from other people because you won't recognise your own most common mistakes. I was always being told off for "And" and "But" starting sentences. Also I have a habit of creating very long run-on sentences. I have a friend whose common mistake is getting the auxiliary verb to be in the singular when it should be in the plural and vice versa. We can argue that it's stylistic but in many cases our mistakes are just irritating to the reader. To be very honest here I know I should have an editor but I can't afford one and that's that. However here is another unconsidered upside to self-publishing - that you can re-edit at a later date.

American English vs British English?

As you're getting on to first and second drafts you need to go back to your audience again. Are you aiming to sell more to British English speakers or Americans?

We have decided to start titling our books for the American market but to write in my normal English voice. There is a really good reason for this. My KDP analytics show that the greatest proportion of my readership are Americans, with British readers coming second, Germans third and Others coming in at just a few percent. Clearly, especially for my book on mould making techniques "Simple Mold

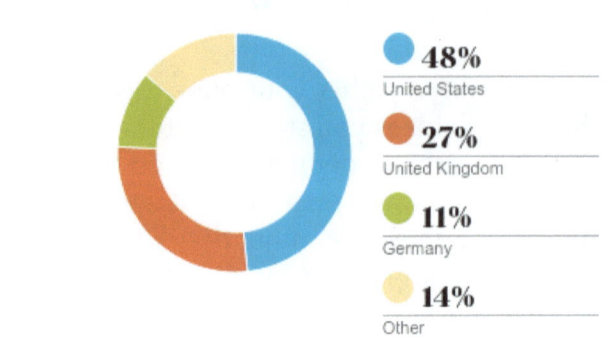

KDP report breakdown showing regions

Making", it makes sense to use the American spelling mold on the cover so they can find it when looking for books on the subject. But my customers mostly know I'm a Brit and I explain in the intro for those who don't that I will be using my natural British English throughout the book. If this is your first book you won't have these analytics so you'll have to look at the balance of your followers on social media and the people who have already shown intention to buy.

Front and end matter

Front matter are the introductory pages before the actual introduction. They might include a pair of illustrated pages. They will certainly include a title page and then a publishing data page; which may also contain copyright information and any disclaimers. You can look at the front matter of this book to find a sample of these. You might have a dedication here or on a separate page, and you will then almost certainly have a contents page.

"End matter" is what they call the last few pages of the book which might contain a glossary/index, a bio, sources and resources. acknowledgements and adverts for you and your other products/publications will also typically be at the back.

Sources and resources

It helps your reader if you give addresses for items that are difficult to source. It also makes you friends in the outside world or is a way of acknowledging special support from a supplier. People are always happy to be given this information and it only takes you a day to get this page done and may gain you several good reviews. People hate searching for tools and materials. You'll be solving that problem for them, and they'll be grateful for it. If you have a popular website, you can join affiliate programs and send your readers there. You are helping them, and it won't cost them any more but you may get a small income from it. (Always let people know if you are sending them to an affiliate page, though.) You might perhaps want to recommend further reading on a subject you don't and won't be covering.

Thanks and acknowledgements

In this section which usually comes just before your author biog, you can thank anyone who has given support or assistance during the writing process. This can include family, friends, mentors, editors, beta readers, agents, or anyone who has contributed to the creation of your book in some way. You can also acknowledge any sources of inspiration or material you may have used, such as books, articles, or interviews. It's your choice who you want to thank, but it's always a good idea to show gratitude to those who have helped or inspired you along the way.

Funnily enough, giving credit does not take away from your kudos for the hard work you put into your book, into learning your skills and adapting other people's ideas to make them your own and your own skills as a teacher. On the contrary, people will know from your generous and appreciative mentions that you are a thoroughly good soul and will love learning from you. And those who you have thanked will get that nice warm feeling of having been of some use.

Also do remember that people don't only buy one tutorial nor one book so you aren't giving away your own book sales by speaking glowingly about someone else's work when it has inspired you. You are augmenting your community. Good relations with other authors/tutors are priceless, since they will quote, reference and share your work if they like it, and if they like you. Some don't want to be part of that kind of mutual support. You can draw your own conclusions about that.

Self-publish with assistance, or find a publisher?

You have finished a book. Congratulations!

We have looked at this question earlier and feel ready to self-publish. However this is a good time to look again at whether you feel competent to do all the additional work or whether you can afford to have it done for you. The cost of publishing yourself or having assistance is comparable except that with self-pub you are investing time rather than money. If you have the money to get an editor, a cover designer and buy in marketing services, as long as you do enough work to find that those services are recommended and diligent, it can be a sensible choice simply because a specialist will do a better job more quickly. But you can do it all yourself.

You can upload and start selling your book for nothing on Amazon. And, if you wait for an offer, nothing on Ingram Spark either.

I've been reading recently about people who have encountered so-called publishers or self-publishers. One first time author was convinced a publisher loved her book and was just asking on Facebook, whether she should go ahead given that her publisher wanted 4 thousand from her and she was disabled. There were lots of replies including people who thought they were helping suggesting slightly cheaper 'publishers'. Some of course, to put it kindly, had been 'vanity pressed' themselves. Yes 4 thousand might well be the cost of doing all that additional work. But have you looked at your probable return on a first book? Be clear whether you are publishing for yourself or to make an income.

These businesses are not traditional publishers. These are actually author services with printers, or links to printers, acting as publishers. Their M.O. is to lead the you, the author, to believe that they have chosen your wonderful work from a pile of not so wonderful. Please, don't be fooled. They will choose anyone who has the money and something which looks like a book. Some will pick and choose those which will make their brand look good from those which won't but they are still not making the investment themselves. You are. They won't really care if you don't sell a book. They might charge you even more for marketing services too. A good version of this hybrid model will make it very clear who and what they are and what they offer and will not play on your ego.

A traditional publisher does not ask you for thousands of pounds. Not one penny in fact. They pay an advance in the hope of earning rather a lot back in the long term (which they did on my first two books). See the beginning of this book where I talk about the pros and cons. Getting a publishing deal is one thing, paying for over-priced author services calling themselves publishers is another. This makes me really angry and sad for those whose dreams are about to be crushed. Be clear what you want and what you need. Either go with a proper traditional publisher if you can get your book accepted, or decide to do it yourself and do due diligence on any publishing services you are offered. We tend to do it all ourselves (well Frank does the important bits for me).

If you're sure it's a great book but needs extra author services, editing, layout, proof reading etc. you can buy in these services individually. Simply laying out a finished book can take just a few hours if everything is prepared in advance. It will cost hundreds, not thousands. Editing is more expensive but still more likely to cost hundreds, not thousands. Translation may cost thousands. Advertising can cost serious money, but a DIY approach to that can also be successful.

Remember that the whole of the publishing world has changed and almost all publishing houses sell a large proportion of their books through Amazon now, so you can even be competing with your own books on Amazon. This means you have a nearer-equal access to the marketplace compared with traditional publishers.

Editing and other Author Services

What author services are out there and what should they cost?

I used Chat GPT to generate these author services costs 1-6 using the question above and I have left them in the dollar format produced by AI. I added number 7 as those are the services I'm most likely to, and have actually used, myself.

1. Book editing: professional editors typically charge by the word or by the hour, with rates ranging from around $0.02 to $0.10 per word, or $40 to $80 per hour.

2. Book cover design: freelance book cover designers may charge anywhere from $50 to $150 per hour, with an average cost of around $100 per hour.

3. Book formatting: book formatting services can cost anywhere from $25 to $100 per hour, depending on the complexity of the project.

4. Ghostwriting: ghostwriters typically charge by the word or by the project, with rates ranging from around $0.10 to $1.00 per word, or $5,000 to $20,000 for a full-length book.

5. Author coaching: author coaches may charge anywhere from $50 to $300 per hour, depending on their level of experience and expertise.

6. Book marketing: book marketing services can vary widely in cost, depending on the type and scope of the service. Some services charge a flat fee, while others may charge an hourly rate, with rates ranging from around $50 to $300 per hour.

7. Social media: marketing support and virtual assistants will generally work from 30 dollars an hour upwards.

Keep in mind that these rates are just general estimates mostly taken directly from an AI answer and the actual cost of author services can vary depending on the provider's level of experience, the complexity of the project, and the specific services. Do your research and get quotes from several providers to find the best fit for your needs and budget.

What are you selling?
It's worth remembering that as a craft author you aren't just giving a story as a novelist does but you are giving the ability to do what you do. That's a genie out of the bottle which cannot be put back in. You are providing the shortcuts from your own learning and often the ability for your reader to make money from your ideas. You need to be paid for that knowledge! So please don't undervalue the years you spent gaining it.

Also remember how much time and/or money you put into the project and how many books you'll have to sell to make your time back and in what timescale you need it to come back in. Remember you are very unlikely to make your money back on a first self-published book, so it has to be part of a longer term strategy.

By the way, publishing a book doesn't stop you selling separate PDFs, quite the reverse. You can even sell the ones out of the book as long as you make it clear to the customers that they are the same ones.

First thoughts on pricing

How to price your book working backwards.

Get an estimate of the print cost of your book and then look at the formulae.

Simple Amazon type formula
You get approximately half of the difference after deducting the book print cost, on simple retail sales online through Amazon.

Ebook pricing is similar. There's no printing cost but they charge a download cost per megabyte.

Simple Ingram Spark type formula
We used to set the price to get 2 euros per book until just recently. These days we are more likely to double that unless the book has a specific marketing motive. We try to keep those books down in price both to encourage sales, and quite honestly it feels morally right to do so. We did decide to get a better return on one of our books that does have a sales side to it, but this is because we knew the market could stand it, as comparable books were selling at the higher prices. In some cases we'll even market at a fiver profit from each book. It really is nice to see those passive fivers ticking up.

Part 7: More marketing. Pre-publication strategies

Title and design of your book cover

It's amazing how many authors think that the contents of their book sell it. However, that's not entirely true. First, people have to see the book, think it looks good, and only then will they read the back blurb or the book's description. Afterward, they'll take a look at the reviews. So, it's no good having a splendid book but a poor cover or a great cover and a disappointing book. The two have to match. That way the reader buys the book, gets what they expect, or more, and reviews your book accordingly. Let's assume you've written a great book though. Of course, you have! Then, you need a great title on the cover to go with it. The only way to attract customers, is to tell them exactly what's in the book by the content and style of your cover. The back blurb should focus on their first impression and make them hit "buy now". We will deal with the design of your cover in the design and layout sections of this book but now you need a snappy title. It stands to reason your title should reflect the contents of your book. If you can make it a little intriguing too, that's bonus interest points.

We've chosen to use the words "How To" in the title of this book because we want to make it very clear that it's just that. It tells you how to do something. Other craft and hobby books may take a different approach.

How a subtitle can help you sell a book

Look at the title "Big Book of a Miniature House" by Christine-Lea Frisoni (a bestseller) which has the subtitle - "Create and Decorate a Dolls House Room by Room". The title itself is catchy and intriguing, but it wouldn't infer that it's a tutorial book. The subtitle clears that up and makes it absolutely clear what those tutorials will teach without even using the words "how to".

Subtitles can be a powerful marketing tool that can help sell a book in several ways.

Clarification: a subtitle can make the contents of the book more obvious. It can help readers to decide whether the book is something that they would be interested in reading.

Differentiation: a good subtitle can help a book to stand out from other similar books in the market. Emphasising the unique angle or benefit of the book, making it more appealing to potential readers who are looking for something new or different or even something they didn't even know they were looking for.

Targeting: a carefully crafted subtitle can help the author to target a specific audience. By including keywords or phrases that are relevant to the target audience, the author can attract the attention of readers who are more likely to be interested in the book.

SEO: your subtitle can also be used to improve visibility in online searches. By including relevant keywords in the subtitle, your book is more likely to appear in search results when readers are looking for books on a particular topic.

Choosing Categories and Keywords

My suggestion is that you get yourself a spreadsheet to put all this information into.

You should know from your early research into comparable books where your book fits in the categories. Go to your favourite comparable book now and go down to the categories the book is ranked in. Click on the best ranking of those categories. And on the side, next to the top 100 books you will see the "path" taken.

For example in this case we have:

⟨ Any Department

⟨ Books

⟨ Crafts, Hobbies & Home

⟨ Crafts & Hobbies

Toys & Models

Dollhouses

You can choose that path and enter it into your spreadsheet in this format (note > arrows):

Books > Crafts, Hobbies & Home > Crafts & Hobbies > Toys and Models > Dollhouses

Save these along with any others you discover that look right for your book's niche. It may be that you want to choose different categories. Your comparable author may not have chosen the very best category to be found in or to rank in. Keep looking at other popular books which compare with yours and see what other categories they are ranking in. Choose 10 different possibilities if you can but put the favourite ones in the first 2 as those will be the ones you will actually use on publication.

Unfortunately it's not even that simple. All regions have different category paths both for print and for Kindle. Some regions don't have a path that another one does. For example there's no polymer clay category in the UK whereas in the US and Canada there is. So choose the first two wisely. There will be an opportunity to add more categories later after publication so that's the reason for collecting the extra ones.

You will also need to choose some keywords or phrases for Amazon in advance of publication. It's important to sprinkle keywords throughout the blurb and introductions to your book.

Choosing the right keywords can help improve its visibility on Amazon itself as Amazon does function like a search engine. Making sure the right descriptive words appear in your blurb will help it be found on other search engines and online marketplaces, making it easier for your readers to find and purchase your book.

"How do I choose effective keywords and phrases?"

Start by making a list of words and phrases that best describe your book. This can include the genres one of which might be "craft book". Then you will drill down into the niche. Think about what readers might search for when looking for a book like yours.

Think about the specific techniques, materials, and projects that are featured in your book. Brainstorm a list of relevant terms, such as knitting, crocheting, paper crafts, woodworking, jewellery making and so on.

Next, consider the audience for your book. Who is most likely to be interested in your craft or hobby? What search terms might they use to find books like yours? For example, if your book is aimed at beginners, you might want to include keywords like "easy", "simple" or "beginner-friendly".

You should also research the keywords that are commonly used in your niche. Look at similar books and see what keywords they use in their titles, subtitles, and descriptions. Use tools like Google Keyword Planner or Amazon's search bar to find related keywords and phrases that have high search volume and low competition.

Use long-tail keywords: long-tail keywords are more specific phrases that can help narrow down your book's audience. For example, instead of using a broad keyword like "craft book" use a more niche phrase like for example "polymer clay dollhouse miniatures".

Make sure that the keywords, or rather keyphrases you select are appropriate and precise. Avoid using misleading or irrelevant keywords, as this can lead to unfavourable reviews if people buy your book and find it isn't at all what they expected. Make it easy for your reader to buy a book they love by identifying those buyers and creating the connection by the precision and descriptiveness of your keyword choices. It's really worth taking time to do this research.

Descriptions can be generated from these keywords and phrases. Having said that, I have heard that if you repeat the same keywords in the description on Amazon, you are wasting extra findability. So use some of your keywords to produce your description, and some as Amazon keywords.

"Hot launch"

The aim of a hot launch is to get your book high into the rankings.

If you are starting to have confidence that you will get it finished you'll probably also be confident in looking at your community for your early buyers. You need to build your community of potential buyers and of course reviewers well in advance. These buyers will form the basis of the rankings for your books. They will provide early reviews and ratings and because they are motivated buyers, their reviews are likely to be good ones.

Because it was in a different genre, and under a pen name, I didn't have the confidence to do that with my Frugalist book and so I had a cold launch. Which is not a great place to start. It languished with very few sales for over a year which was a shame because it is a good and informative book for its audience. You can come back from a flop but it takes some doing and some investment. I forgot the golden rule to build up my community of potential buyers well in advance.

Because I had a magazine column, and was doing live classes, before my first book came out I had a thousand books already sold. (In the form of names of rock solid buyers). I simply had to email each person and ask them to call me with their card details or send me a cheque (yes they used them in those days) then slap their address labels on big envelopes and stuff the contents of several boxes of books into the envelopes. That was what I'd call a Hot Launch! And within a month or two I'd sold another thousand. This was good because I really needed it! After all, It was 3 years since I'd started writing the book. It did help to make that book an instant bestseller in its field and it stayed in the bestsellers for many, many years and still sells now. The second one did almost as well.

These days it ought to be even easier, but sometimes it seems harder. These days fewer of your books will pass through your own hands unless you really put the footwork in so you do need to plan. Make a list of any live appearances you are going to, before the book comes out. Are you giving any classes? - be prepared with marketing materials and hustle. At craft fairs that you're appearing at, have a form where people can give you permission to contact them by email or social media. When talking about your upcoming book on social media say "please comment if you want me to let you know when the book is released". And do drive people to sign up for your mailing list either in a superfan category or in a books only category. Make sure people are expecting and looking forward to your contact and, of course, your new book. People love to support

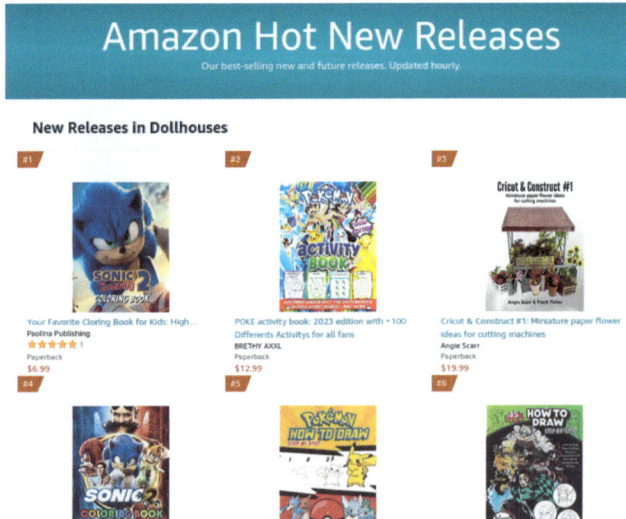

and they love to be first. Let those first buyers know that you appreciate them.

Of course it's easy enough for me to get a good handful of buyers at launch for one of my craft books. But it's nothing like those heady days when I appeared in magazines and at miniatures fairs and gave classes. And of course what I was presenting was, at the time, a relatively new technique to the miniatures market. Certainly I know that my craft books still won't fall on entirely stony ground. But of course that isn't just luck. I was lucky I'd thought to send my early videos to Marion Fancey (then publisher of DHMS). But you create that kind of luck. Specialist magazines are always looking for great content. Offer them early content from the book. Try and time it so that the magazine comes out in the month before the book. Don't worry about the layout of your project. The magazine will do that for you. Make sure you tell them not to republish anywhere without your permission and make sure they add your contact details to the bottom of your piece. You may not get paid. If you do, the standard rate is around 75 pounds (in the UK) per page. It hasn't gone up in 20 years as distribution has fallen.

Now of course we have social media which is a whole different and potentially bigger pool, but you also have much bigger competition than I did back then.

Lots of authors blog, YouTube and TikTok. Personally I find video challenging but it absolutely does work, whether its advance tutorials or a flick through of your book proof as soon as it arrives.

If you want a task for this stage of your journey I'd say spend some more time collecting the customers that you have and finding new ones. So if you are working with a folder, write down all the places you are already going to find customers. Make yourself a database, if you don't already have one, of friends to contact as you are getting towards the end of writing the book. Have a sheet of names of friends who have already promised to buy and review and hold them to it. Put it in the back of your folder and scribble every single name of everybody who says they are interested because they may seem like just one person to you but they are the most important readers you will ever have. They are more important than the income. They are the beginning of a "hot" algorithm if they go through Amazon. And if you can get the ball rolling early on it will continue to roll. Learn not to be shy or embarrassed at asking friends and relatives to actually support you by buying on the very first day. Now I don't love Amazon to bits but we are playing ball in that park these days so you can't afford to ignore the Amazon algorithms if you want success. We'll talk about publishing on other platforms too later on.

After you've written down the names of every family member, friend, past customer etc. you can rely on, you now need to look at augmenting your potential reach. This is all about building your communities. It's about joining the groups and being helpful, respectful and not spamming. I do know people who take a short term spammy approach to advertising and I must admit I shut their chatter out almost instantly, even if their work is good.

We aren't on the internet for a constant barrage of adverts but we will buy from people whose work we like or just people we like! You will earn more respect and more long term customers by posting helpful replies to other people's posts than you will putting adverts and nothing else on the pages. Also when you do reply to questions etc. even if you are the world's authority on a subject, be a bit humble for goodness sake! You don't know that poster's story. And if you come over "the big I am" you really will turn people off. You have to think of groups as like family gatherings. Don't push people around and don't be pushed around. And the old saying "if you can't say anything kind don't say anything at all" really rings true here.

If you haven't already, also join a couple of large Facebook groups today. Identify the most popular ones in your genre or extended genres. You're ideally looking for groups that are relaxed and inclusive but well managed with over 4 thousand members. But a really lovely supportive group with fewer members is just as good. A massive group will give you a further reach but your posts will disappear very quickly. Make sure they are groups that in large proportion are your target audience but don't narrow down too far. I've just joined a group called "Advertise and Sell your Handmade Crafts Community" for example. A pretty good choice as there are 100 thousand members! It's an extended community who may not know of my work yet. I have previously said limit your time on Facebook and I mean it, but you can give yourself that half hour or even an hour a day as useful pre-marketing time. Just know when to stop.

Description

When publishing on Amazon your book description is one of the most important marketing tools you have. So I suggest you write this out in full first and then distil the most important points into your back cover text

Hook: start with a hook that captures readers' attention and piques their interest. It could tell the reader what reading the book will do for them. How it will solve any problems they have. It might do that in the form of a question such as "Have you ever thought of writing a craft book and don't know where to start?". You could write several of these in a row. These questions can form the trigger for the explanation of the benefits your reader will get from buying your book.

Benefits: a brief summary of the book's contents, highlighting the key themes, ideas, and insights that readers can expect to find inside. Make sure to focus on the benefits that readers will gain from reading your book. If your book has any unique features or benefits, such as exercises, illustrations, or templates, highlight them too. This can help pique readers' interest and give them a reason to choose your book over others. You might like to use bullet points for this.

Target Audience: identify the target audience for your book and explain why it is relevant to them. In our case we want to say that this book is especially appropriate for small craft businesses and people with new ideas and techniques to share, reading this book will help you to turn the dream of writing a book into a reality: step-by-step.

Biography: you might include a very brief author biog that highlights your qualifications, experience, or expertise in the subject matter. This can help establish credibility as an author and make readers more likely to trust you to help them with their own creative aspirations.

Testimonials: if you have written another book or taught classes in your field you might add testimonials. We don't usually use these but I think I should. This is no time to be modest! This will help establish your authority.

Call to Action: I find these a little difficult to craft for book descriptions but people with real authority in the publishing sector would suggest that you always include a "buy now" call of some kind. Certainly make your last sentence/s as strong as possible

"If you are a crafter with an idea or technique to share with the world, then this book is the perfect step-by-step guide for you. You'll learn everything you need to know about self-publishing, from writing and photography, through formatting your book to marketing it to the right audience."

For examples look at the sales page on Amazon for this and other books you are interested in. For an example of how the back cover can be written from this look at the back cover of this book. Or the Your Creative Business book.

Part 8: Putting the book together

Photo editing

We have two software suggestions for this. Pay-per-month **Adobe Photoshop**, or free **Krita**. We have always used Photoshop until very recently and are just starting to experiment with Krita.

The most important thing about editing is to start with a picture that is well lit and in focus, (see the earlier section on photography). It is very difficult to rescue a bad shot.

You can place images in the layout as you go along, cropping and positioning them to suit then edit them later. However we feel editing photos as a batch before layout is more efficient and lets you judge standout shots easier. It is also easier to get consistent colouring across a project. If the lighting, or part of it, is from the sun it will change colour subtly throughout the day.

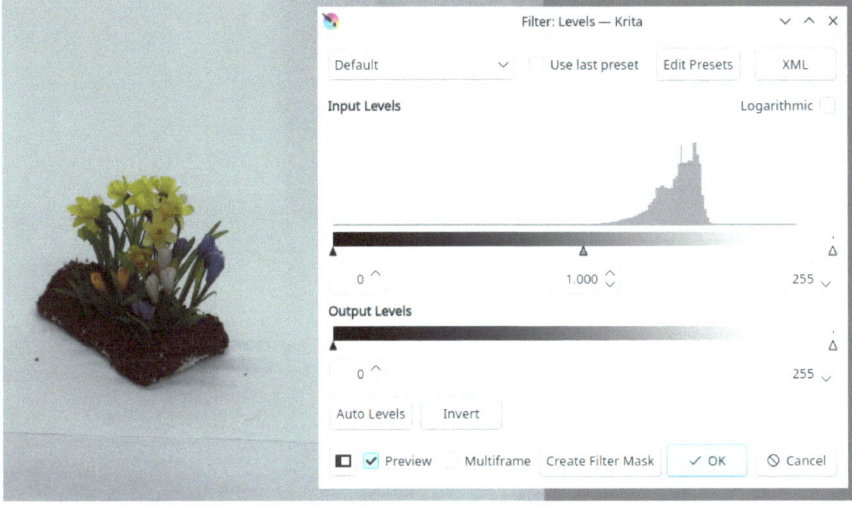
Krita colour levels (before adjustment)

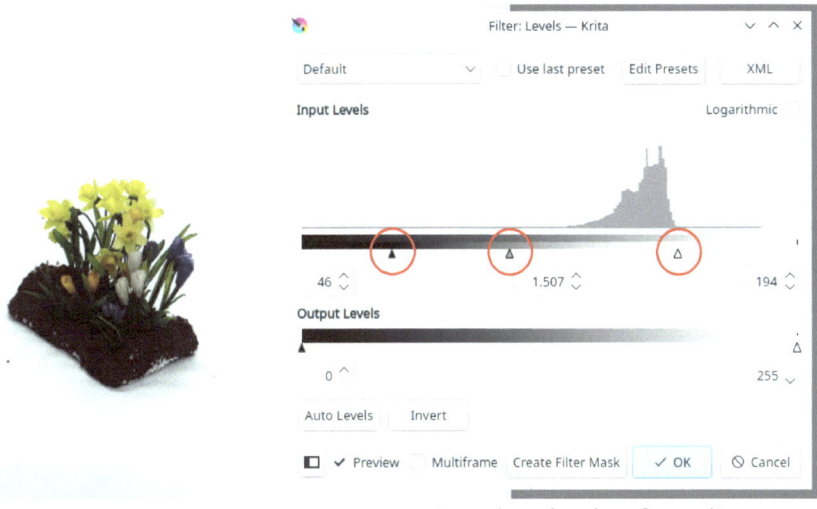
Krita colour levels (after adjustment)

Levels
The simplest tool on an image editing program looks and sounds very complicated but in fact is not as difficult as it seems. It's called the "Levels Histogram". Click on it before you do anything else to the image. You will normally see most of the graph is in the middle with flat or empty sections at the left and right. Almost always the best thing to do is pull the triangular pointer on the right to the start of peak in the graph, similarly the pointer on the left. Then move the middle until you are happy with overall brightness and level of detail.

Photoshop does have an automatic colour feature that will alter the levels for you, but can affect the colour balance too. Often that is a step too far if you have a well-lit photograph against a white background. In cases like this it can tint the image in a way that you might not like.

Colour Balance
If you have to use this tool it normally means something was wrong with the initial lighting, maybe the sun was fading and turning towards red, maybe it clouded over. Here you can tweak the balance of the 3 primary light

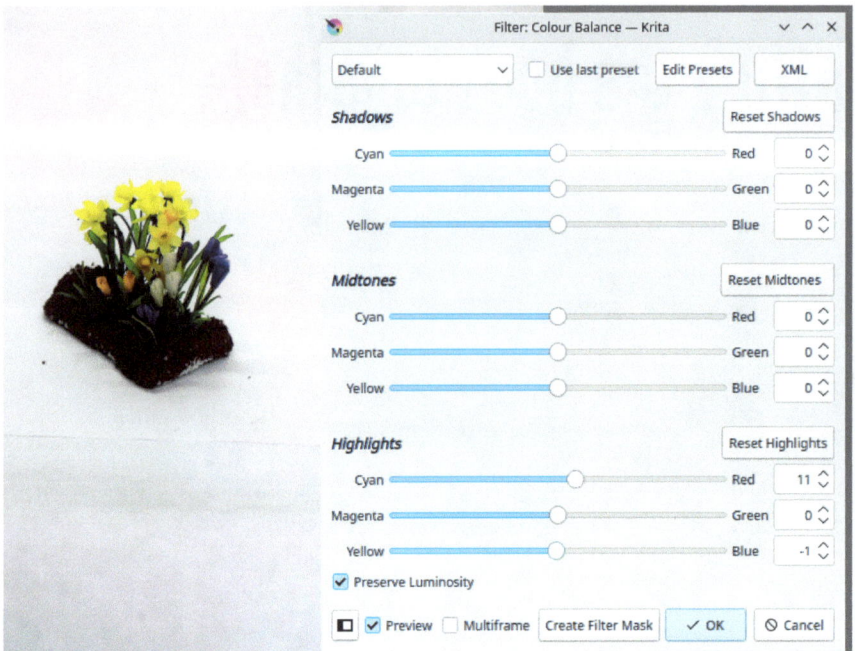

Krita colour balance

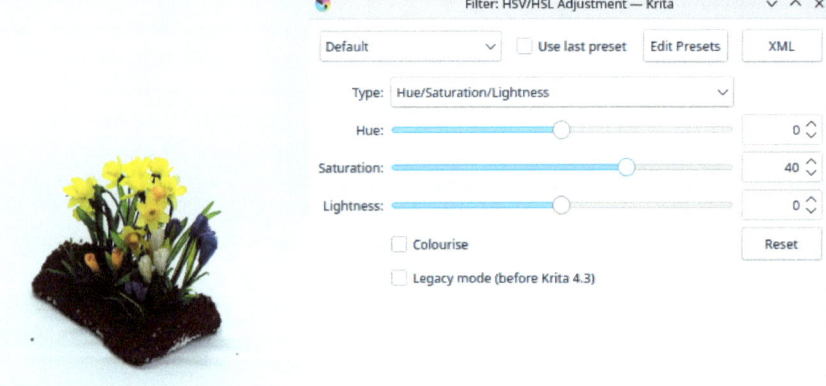

Krita colour saturation

colours against their print "opposites". Often it needs little more than a small move from yellow to blue to put things right.

It's natural for artists more used to mixing colours by adding to find this confusing at first, so play around if you aren't accustomed to this way of thinking about colour and light.

Note: it is well worth making sure your balance is the same across the whole of a step-by-step process, as lighting at different times of day can change the colour. This can be especially obvious when your hands are in the shot and you have a sequence taken across a period of time when it can change skin colour.

Saturation

If your photo looks washed out (maybe too much light) you can try to get a little of the strength back. Saturation will push colour back into the picture rather than brightening or darkening it as Brightness or Contrast would.

This is also useful for adding extra power to a cover image or an advert.

Cutout

By far the best thing (in our opinion) you can do to an image is to cut it out. It immediately becomes stronger and has more presence.

This is a multi stage process refining the selection to be perfect. The first selection tool to use is the "magic wand" which I set to "25" which is the measure of how similar a colour should be included. Also click "additive" so you add each selection to the existing ones.

Krita settings for "magic wand"

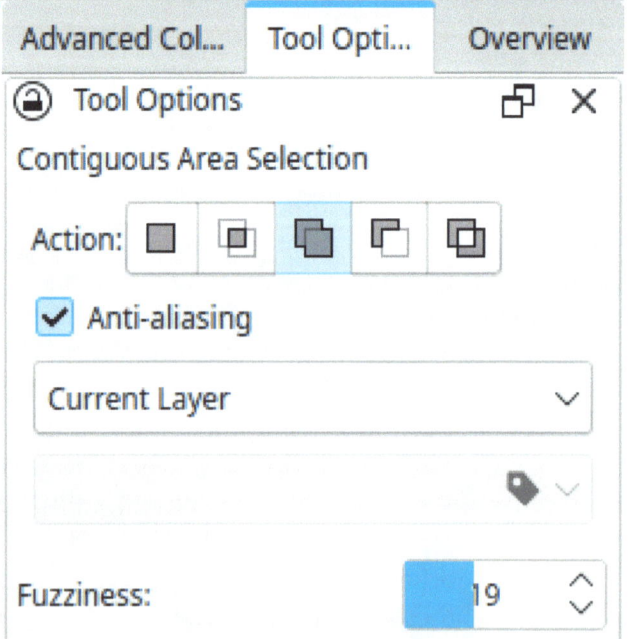

Krita multiple selection - you will see moving dots around the outline

Click on the white bits, you will find they are several shades of white, click them all. If you have been lucky you are finished. Normally, though, you will see that you have to add the gaps in between leaves or flowers, or spokes in a wheel etc. I then zoom and add them in to the selection, always checking I haven't accidentally added in areas I don't want to cut. If it happens I turn the setting down to "10" and go again. If that fails I move on to the Lasso or Freehand selection tool which lets you draw or exclude selections by hand.

The next step is to clear all your selection to white and look at the edges before deselecting. If the edges are rough I can extend the selection by 3-5 pixels and use Gaussian Blur to fade them into the white background.

Finally Deselect and use the Unsharp Mask checking the amount and distance until you are happy with the sharp image. Don't do too much or you will see obvious grain in the image.

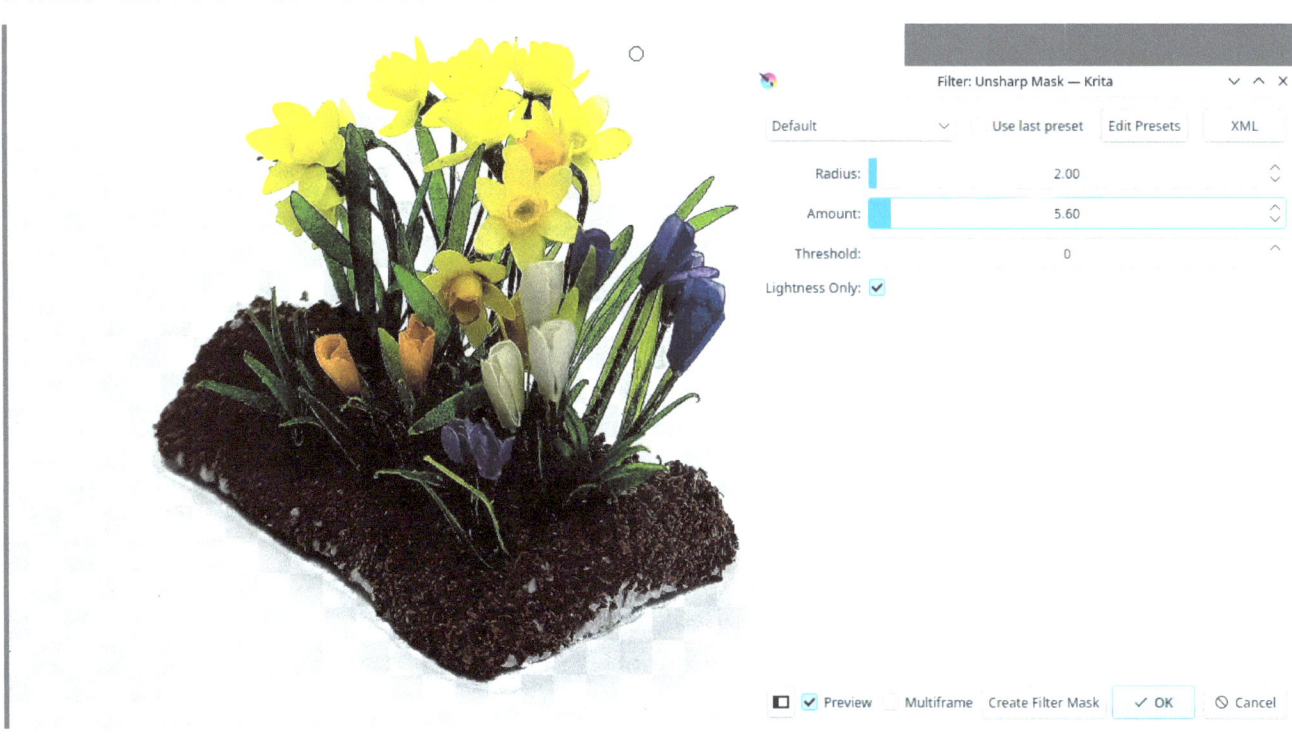

Krita unsharp mask

Layout

We have two suggestions for layout programs. There are obviously others depending on your hardware. Our recommendations based on experience are the pay-per-month **Adobe InDesign** (Windows & Mac) or **Scribus** (Windows, Mac, Linux, Chromebook) which is free.

We don't intend to take you step by step on learning the software, detailed paid and free tutorials are available online. This guide will show you what to do with the software once you are comfortable with it.

InDesign

This can be hired per month. If you only need it at the end of the project we recommend getting all the text and images together, checked and processed first. This also saves production costs. InDesign is a well established, stable and very capable piece of software that will do the print layout and a decent amount of the work towards making an ebook for you at the click of a menu. However it only runs on Windows and Mac. You are also tied to their updates and feature changes, with little control.

Scribus

Scribus is a little more scrappy, has a few less features, but runs on Windows, Mac, Chromebook and Linux. Most of all it is totally free so you can work with it all the way through the project if you intend to work page by page.

View mode

I recommend working in "facing pages" mode as you create the documents, but when you export the final it must be single pages. Also watch out for bleed images from facing pages crossing over into the bleed of the matching page when you export (see page 58).

Chapter structure and multiple files

With any layout software it's not advisable to have more than a handful of pages in a single document if you intend to lay several images per page as we do on our step-by-step projects. The memory use and processing time increases massively if you do, as the software tries to re-set the text flow many pages ahead in the document even as you correct a single word. More often than not this causes slowdowns, and eventually crashes, as you push the memory in use to the limit.

The best approach is to break the book down into not only chapters but sections in the chapters. With InDesign you hold all these together in a document called a "book". This

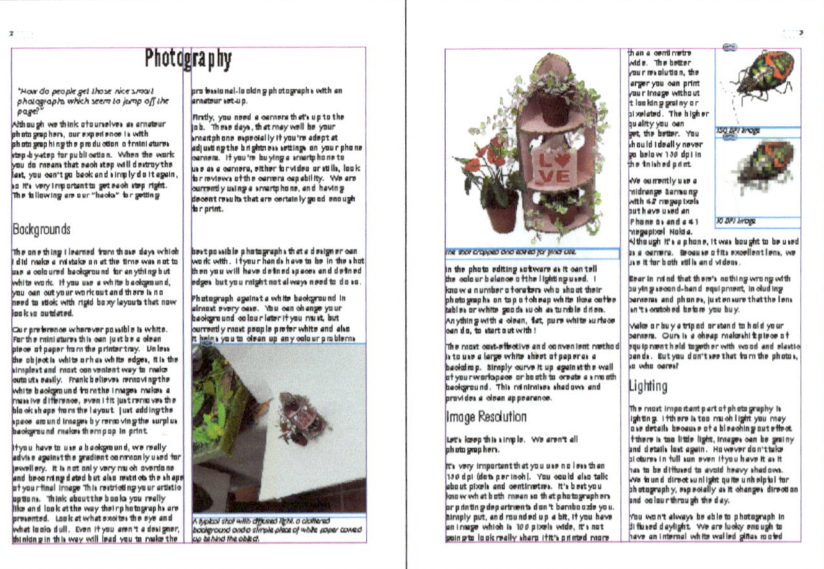

InDesign facing pages view

InDesign book document

book doesn't deal with the shape or layout of pages, styles or margins, solely the linked documents and their page numbers. It can do "pre-flight" checks on the full contents to make sure all images are in place and current in the pages before you create a PDF. For example if you update an image, the program will remind you to replace old copies. InDesign can also export all the separate elements in editable format. That is to say it can make the whole package of text, fonts and images for sending to a print company or external designer. This can be useful if you need additional work done by someone else. When you are ready it can also create a single PDF for print or upload.

Scribus is less sophisticated and relies on you making a batch of final PDFs for each section of pages then glueing the PDFs together into one document.

Takeaway

If you intend to produce numerous books regularly, investing in InDesign is a wise decision due to its additional features. However, if you're creating your first book and want to test the waters, Scribus is a free option that you can experiment with for several months.

The basic concepts of both programs, such as styles, frames, and documents, are quite similar, so transitioning between them is relatively effortless.

Inner layout design

Page size and colour or B/W

We made a mistake with our Your Creative Business book when we first published it in a small format because Print On Demand companies charge the same per page whatever the size of paper. Our book being smaller meant a lot more pages. We had also decided on colour even though there weren't a lot of coloured pages in it. Both those decisions were a mistake in hindsight. Our target customers are people who are starting out or struggling in craft businesses and very few of these will want to pay out for an expensive book, no matter how beautiful. We reformatted it to a large page size and changed it to monochrome. This slashed the costs by two thirds. We called it "The Starving Artist Edition". Not only was the new format half price but it made us twice as much profit. We like to give value so we use the available page space to lower the number of pages needed. This can also increase your potential profit. Up to a point. You do however want a nice open layout that's easy to read and sections that are well separated. I don't think that customers like a lot of empty pages if they don't have an obvious function.

However If you are planning to post books a smaller page size will save a lot of costs on postage and envelopes. With a craft book

InDesign page setup

InDesign master page

full of images customers may be less likely to enjoy the smaller text, complain about smaller images and think maybe the book isn't worth the money. We found this with our small version of The Colour Book. It had as much content as our larger books but just felt less impressive in the hand. We later changed this one to full size too.

Master

This isn't a real page, it is where you define how all pages will look. All your margin choices, page numbers etc. go in here. In InDesign if you mess a page up you can "Apply Master Page" and put it all back again over your existing text and images.

I then also define all the styles etc. and save the page as a template so that all future pages are the same standard design.

Bleed

A technical sounding item but something to think about before you place your first image on a page. Bleed is basically letting an image overrun the page, so if you want something to carry on right to the very edge it has to go slightly over (3.2mm or 1/8th inch seems the new standard). This way when the page is cut to size and glued in the book there won't be a white line where the cut was very slightly out of line.

It also lets you do dramatic title pages, or images taking a shape in the bottom corner, or many other layout options to take away from the fixed shape of the page.

Title pages

Title pages - 2 page spread

A chapter can start with a full page or even double page picture and a title. This is just "eye candy" but makes the whole book more enjoyable and impressive.

Use bleed to get the full amount of image in, and leave space around it for the title.

InDesign page bleed - the red outer lines

Margins

Margins are important and depend on the number of pages in the book but must always have a bigger "inner" margin where the book is glued and content won't be visible if you don't leave enough space. You can also have extra height where you choose to put the page numbers. Smaller margins make the book feel cramped so my recommendation is to not scrimp on them. 25mm / 1 inch inner is good unless your book has hundreds of pages. Slightly less for the outer and bottom (if you are numbering at the top).

InDesign page margins

Columns

There is a standard in print that a column should be approximately 40 characters in your standard reading font. It is rare that a full size book will read well if you go fully across the page with more than 60 characters.

I normally go with 2 columns but may adjust that if I have a column of images. Maybe the images will take up half, one third or even two thirds of the width of the page. If the text is below 40 characters in a column I will not select justified but instead use left aligned and leave it with a ragged right edge. See 'Body' later in this section for alignment choices.

Page numbering

If making a simple craft how-to book there is little need for anything other than a page number at the top of the page, aligned to the left of the text column at the outer edge. Normally a book will have double page layout, with even numbers at the left, odd at the right. You can add section or chapter text in the header, but I normally choose not to.

The software will have a 'special character' for page numbers that you put into your Master page and then when you state what the document start page number is, this will change and count automatically from there.

Styles

Layout software gives powerful style attributes that can be changed across the entire document at any time. This is the standard way to work and can apply across the whole book with one click in InDesign

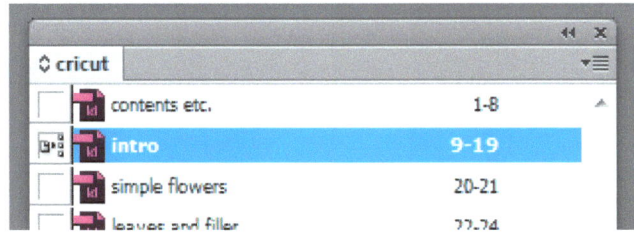

InDesign showing Intro as the standard stylesheet

The best way to save yourself lots of wasted work is to fix the following styles before putting the book together, that way it will be consistent from the first page. Make up multiple options, trying different alignments, fonts and spacing before starting the work proper. You can import selected styles into your documents if you change your mind later but it will affect the layouts you have already made.

Font choices

The big thing about fonts is you can only get away with about 3 on a page without looking weird or amateurish. Also different fonts are designed for different purposes. Something useful for the main body of text will be less impressive as a large heading, as it won't have much weight to it.

If you are thinking of using Comic Sans or similar, or some kind of 'brush script' you probably shouldn't. They are mostly used for making quick posters and get tiring to read pretty quickly.

Analysing

Use a graphics program like Inkscape which is free and runs on Mac, Linux and Windows. We use Corel Draw but we're old! You can stay within the design software of your machine but we find that restrictive.

Example Gill Sans as body text

Analysing

Use a graphics program like Inkscape which is free and runs on Mac, Linux and Windows. We use Corel Draw but we're old! You can stay within the design software of your machine but we find that restrictive.

Example Optima as body text

Analysing

Use a graphics program like Inkscape which is free and runs on Mac, Linux and Windows. We use Corel Draw but we're old! You can stay within the design software of your machine but we find that restrictive.

Example serif font as body text

Body

The people I have worked with in the past often attempt to cram a huge amount of text into a small space. This drew me to the font Gill Sans for the body of text. In less cramped settings I like the openness and space that Optima gives and I used it in this book. Both are sans-serif fonts as I find that serif fonts need to be proportionally bigger to be readable at the same font size due to the decoration added to the basic letter shapes. However both Gill Sans and Optima have slightly more detail than plain Helvetica.

Next, as discussed on the previous page, you need to work out if you have enough column width to get a reliable fully justified column of text, meaning it has a straight edge left and right. If you have fewer than 40 characters, or do wrapping around images, it will become forced and the spacing will be odd looking. In smaller widths I normally choose left justified text, meaning it has a ragged edge at the right.

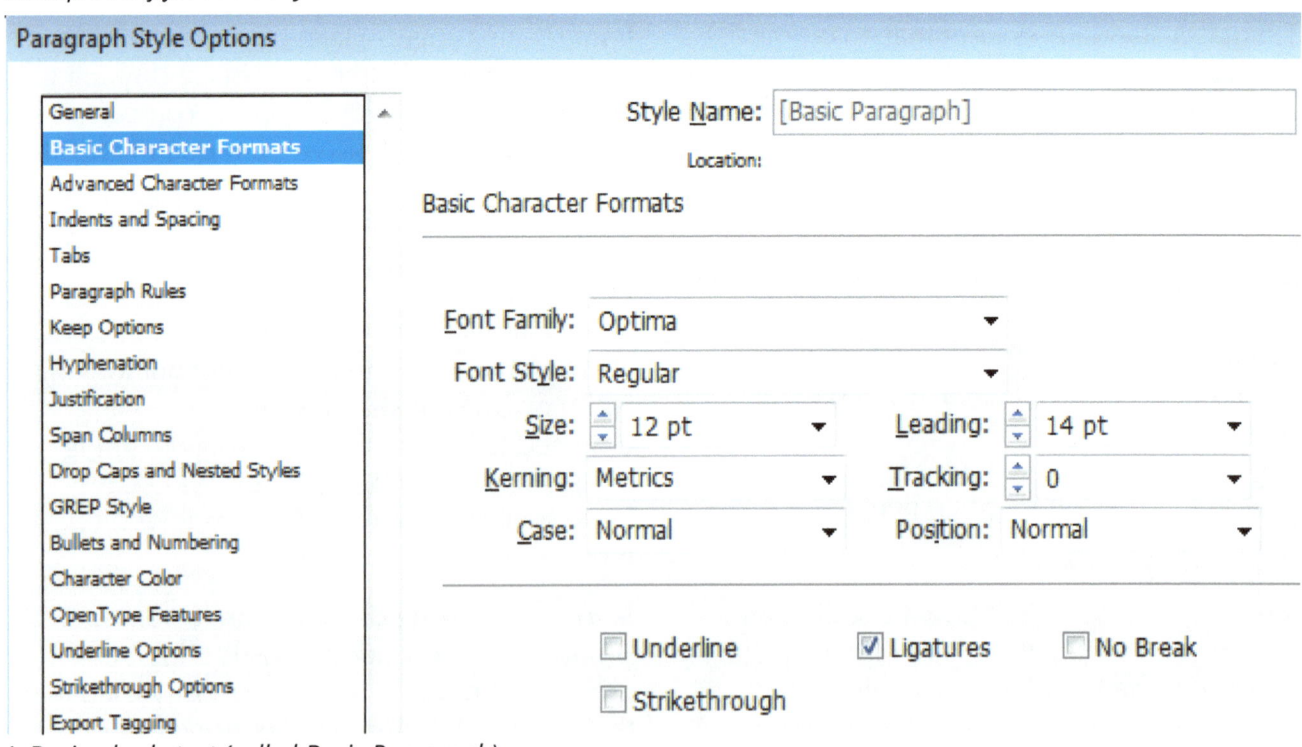

InDesign body text (called Basic Paragraph)

League Gothic

Museo

Titles

The title is a big statement at the start of a section or on the cover. Fonts tend to be heavier or bold, and centred.

You may make a style choice to underline the title to make a break from the text, though I would use the 'line' or 'paragraph rule' feature of the paragraph settings rather than the plain underline of the font. That way you can add space before and after the line.

My favourites for this are League Gothic or Museo (in a heavier weight).

Headings

Similar to title but smaller, used at the start of a section. Could be left aligned or centred. Spacing after is helpful to mark out the break into a new subject, especially if it is running on the same page as a previous subject.

Futura Md

Subheadings

Normally smaller still and left aligned. This breaks up a subject into smaller chunks.

My favourites for this are Futura Md or League Gothic.

Open sans

Futura Lt

Italics and captions

Maybe justified or left, could be indented in from both sides used for a quote or an information box. It marks a section that is connected to the subject, or captions an image.

My favourites for this are Open Sans or Futura Lt.

Sectional text flow

Normally you will want to set the template to run text into a new page automatically by default as you add more. The other option is more advanced where you continue pages manually and place them where you need them. This method is from newspaper design where a story might be split across pages as they find space. For a craft book just keep it running from one page to the next unless you have an awkward issue, though it is better to fix the issue so the reader can read in a straight line.

The exception is little snippets of information that relate to the subject but are additional with no strict place in the running order. These can be pulled out and set in their own box, maybe with a line and a faint background colour and their own subheading as we do in this book. Angie opted for this design here to break up large amounts of information in a style that owes a lot to writing for magazines. Important themes, points to note and ways of thinking can be highlighted in this way.

Photo text flow

A craft book may need to place many images alongside the project, hopefully on the same place as the text describing the process. You can number the photos and reference them in the text, or caption the photos underneath.

Your choice of shape will have a big impact on the look of the book. We have been disappointed in the past by publishers just placing several similar size blocks of square photos all the way through the book. You can decide to add more visual interest. If a photo is the final result make it big and show off the work. Likewise if something shows a key process emphasise it. You can still use blocks but stack them in different ways on a page, e.g. on one page you could have them all down one side, on another use them in a triangle at the corner.

As mentioned in the Cutout section freeing the image of all the background around it makes it stand alone much better and even in a block of images this gives a feeling of shape and space.

Note the difference between the two types of text wrap on the right.

'Bleeding lines', simple or complex lines plus Skinner shade to mute the edges.

This is exactly the same process as making a striped skin (see chestnuts above) except that when you cut the slices for a skin and put them together you push at the lines in one direction to cause them to become slightly diagonal thus slightly covering part of the line with the other colour. This works especially well with semi translucent skins as in this garlic cane. It makes the lines slightly more subtle in a similar way to the blended stacking but without all the hard work. And there is a sense of the colour being there, but covered. I think this is a lovely, if a bit subtle, effect.

Lines through shades (strawberry)
This is just adding the 'inserting lines' idea to the Skinner shade technique.

Nature created a true beauty in the strawberry.
See strawberry colour p21.

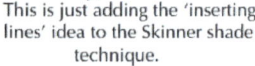
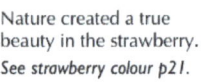

Lines and spots through several layer shades (mackerel)
This project is shown in full on p75 and shows how you can achieve really subtle colour changes plus lines and spots all in the same piece. It's all a matter of taking things step by step and not rushing or taking short cuts.

Simple block text wrapping around images

My most frequently used polymer clay colour techniques

These are the techniques I use because nature throws up these patterns over and over again.

Putting skins on things
This is a simple process and just involves making a really thin even skin (using a pasta machine ensures evenness) around a short fat cylinder of a lighter colour and lengthening it by squeezing and pulling and finally rolling to thin the skin out even more, then closing the ends over on both sides of a small piece to form a small fruit. The thinness and optical lightness of the skin adds realism to what would otherwise simply be a solid blob of clay.
Apple skin colour is Basic Spring Green on p48, add a little more white.

Lines and stripes: chestnuts, onions etc.
Simple lines (stacking). The skin process can be further enhanced by putting stripes into the skin, I use this on onions, rhubarb, garlic and chestnuts (shown). Put simply you make a 2 or 3 (or more) colour sandwich of the colours you need in proportions that will lead you to a pleasing and realistic result *(see cheating and exaggeration p31)*, cut that sandwich and stack up until you get, say, one quarter of the number of lines you need. Then slice and press together the slices to form a skin.

The skin is then put on the centre part, just as in the apples above. In this case, by leaving the end open, I'm using the centre colour as the end colour on the chestnuts.
Chestnut colour is on p82.

Automatic shape text wrapping around images

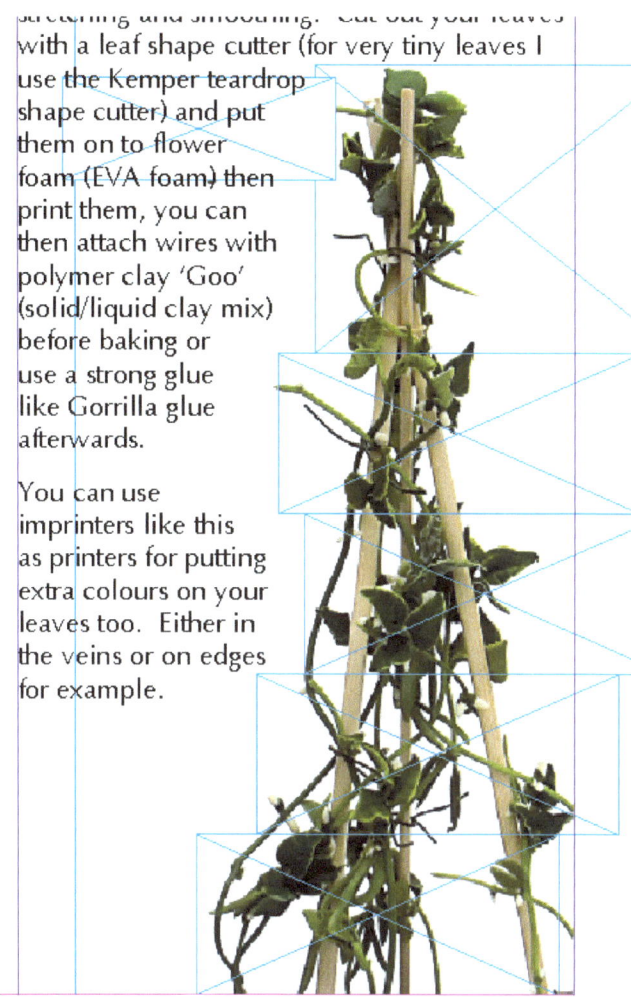

with a leaf shape cutter (for very tiny leaves I use the Kemper teardrop shape cutter) and put them on to flower foam (EVA foam) then print them, you can then attach wires with polymer clay 'Goo' (solid/liquid clay mix) before baking or use a strong glue like Gorrilla glue afterwards.

You can use imprinters like this as printers for putting extra colours on your leaves too. Either in the veins or on edges for example.

Manual shaping text wrapping around images

Normally you will want to run text around an image in some way and there are multiple options.

Simple blocks
Just exclude text from the image. However make sure you have the same margin on each image for consistency.

Also where possible make the gap between subsequent images to side or below match up. The eye registers the organisation from this.

Automatic text flow
Fancier, larger exclusions can be used by automatic settings. Tell the layout software to find the edge of the image (much easier when cut out), then set the same margin of text exclusion as before.

You will often still have to block out a side or a section manually anyway where text is coming in but doesn't fit well.

The automatic method can cause processing and speed issues, possibly stability issues too with larger documents. It does allow for easier moving of images if changing the layout.

Manual shaping
My preferred method after years of experience is just draw empty boxes where you want to exclude the text on larger images. Set these to exclude with your chosen margin and you can box with short, tall, thick or thin boxes in a few seconds to get what you want.

Contents

Indesign has a tool to create a contents page from the entire book based on the styles you select, e.g. Title and Heading. This can be updated at any time. It still needs checking for entries that are not needed or repeated but is a valuable tool. I style it with a tab that is right aligned so the numbers at the end line up properly.

If using Scribus you will need to keep a track manually. As you make each page you can simply copy across the title and page number; it isn't much more work. Only when big changes are made does this go wrong, at which point you need to do a 'sanity check'.

Contents	
Cricut & Construct #1	5
Miniature paper flowers for cutting machines	5
Angie Scarr & Frank Fisher	5
Publishing Data	6
ISBN ???	6
Contents	7
Intro, tools & technique	9
Dollhouse flower scenes for Cricut and other cutters.	9
In this book ...	10
Tools and materials used in this book	10

InDesign automatic contents, simply edit and add styles

Contents	
Intro, tools & technique	9
Tools and materials used in this book	10
Using non-recommended items	12
Copyright issues	12
General cutting advice for miniature floral elements	13
General principles of design for miniatures using Cricut and other cutters	13
My way of working	13
Analysing	14

Contents styled and with right aligned tab

Index

The index is optional, but useful if there is a lot of technical information and many subjects or techniques. Disappointingly I have found little automatic help so far as the software has no idea what is important to the book and overproduces, leaving a lot of work. Manually is simplest. At the end of a project read the finished book and note down topics and page numbers with a comma between each mention. I then put them into a spreadsheet to sort alphabetically and paste them into the index page.

In the same way as you did with the contents list, set a tab. You will probably have to adjust it until you can fit the topic with the most entries in.

baking	*10*
banana	*52*
basic colours	*48*
beans	*18-19,64-66*
bleed	*15,32*
blend	*13,75*
brassica	*67*

Part of the index from Angie Scarr's Colour Book

Advertising pages

To take full advantage of the self-publishing bonus your last page absolutely should contain links to your website, social media and mailing list. Your Patreon or other micropayment page, if you have one, needs to be here too, and links to any courses or classes you are selling. For my first few books I forgot these and that was a serious mistake. You do need to keep people informed at the end of the book. Half your readers won't read right through to your end matter anyway, but they will flick to the last page. Those who do are your superfans and future book buyers.

> Don't waste this opportunity. In the past authors had to slip extra advertising leaflets into their publisher published books at great expense. Now you can just add a page to your book! Where is there a better marketing opportunity?

Also if you have other digital products to sell related to your book they should go here.

This isn't simply cynical and self interested. You are doing a service to your fans letting them know how to get more of what they have obviously loved. If you put it at the very end you can be as blatantly self-promoting as you like. If you don't advertise your other work, you are actually denying your readers knowledge that they want and that they went all the way to the end to get!

Advertising page at the end of the book

ISBNs

Each print book will need an ISBN. This is no more than a 13 digit number of the same sequence used on the barcode on the back of shampoo bottles. However they are a range, e.g. those starting 978 or 979, reserved for book use. Most countries seem to have assigned this to agencies who charge fees that can deter and confuse first time authors with the complexity of applying. After the first time it is a simple transaction to get more.

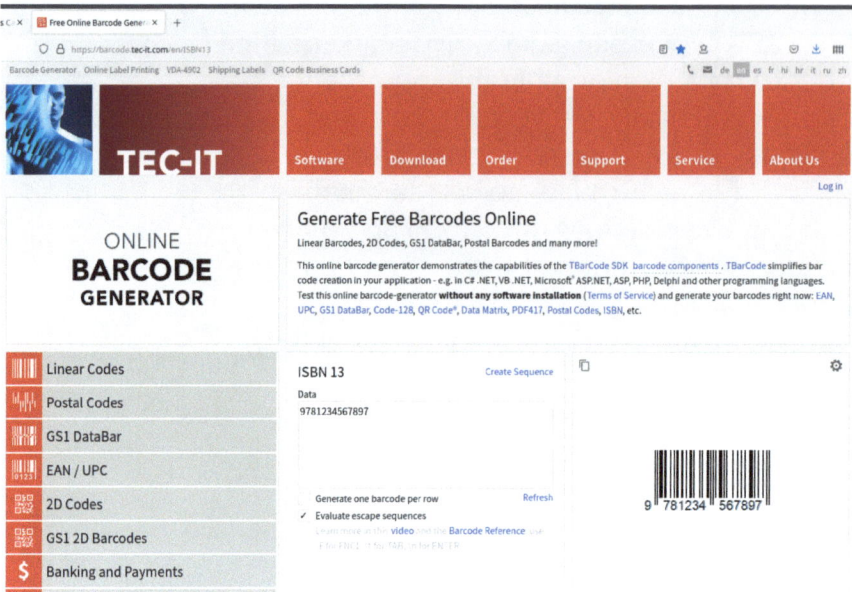

Free barcode generator by Tec-IT

Bought

If you intend to publish lots of books and use Amazon and Ingram or others, bite the bullet and buy some codes from your country's ISBN agency. Long term they cost us under 10 euros a code. Our first code cost 50 euros including registration as a publisher. This is one of the few fixed costs of publishing print books that we accept. We use separate ISBNs for Amazon and Ingram because we don't want to be tied to any one provider. Also some indie bookshops prefer not to do business with Amazon.

Free from Amazon or Ingram

If it is your first book and just a trial then Amazon will give you a free code. Ingram will too in certain countries. However these are tied to the provider.

Barcodes

Many people get confused by the relationship between ISBN and barcode. A barcode is simple a graphic of the ISBN number. Barcodes can be generated free online from your ISBN and downloaded as a graphic. Ignore the option to add a price as it makes no sense when released worldwide in multiple currencies. It also makes things difficult if you want to change the price in the future, especially as Ingram and others can charge you to change your cover or body content.

Amazon will generate the barcode for you and place it in the bottom right of your back cover, so leave space there. They provide a detailed PDF with measurements and placements for the cover which it is essential to follow.

Ingram and others expect you to make the barcode and place it yourself.

e.g. https://barcode.tec-it.com/en/ISBN13

Cover design

Whether you design your own cover or get someone to design it for you there are certain things you need to get right. Nothing says self-published like a badly designed cover. Using Amazon's own cover design tools doesn't usually help much.

We noticed a lot of self-pub authors these days ask around their groups to see which cover they prefer. It can cause a buzz for buying.

Funnily enough on the day we started editing this I got an email in my inbox which said something along the lines of "Thinking of designing your cover ... Don't". There is definitely something to this as we've seen some horrendous self-published book covers. The saddest part of this is when the contents are really good. If you know that some thought needs to go into your layout to appeal to the reader this goes ten times for the cover. It's your actual shop window. Don't, for goodness sake, skimp on this if you can afford a designer.

Here's the thing ... we can't and we aren't industry experts. We do however want to help you to avoid some of the worst mistakes in case you're on a shoestring too. It is very fair to suppose that if you are creative you can come up with good ideas for a cover but for so many it seems to be an "I'm tired now and I just want the book out" afterthought. Perfectly OK if you only want to provide books to friends. And maybe you have a lot of friends and followers. But maybe you want to sell to people who have never discovered you (yet) too.

> Whether you're doing it yourself or are getting someone to do it for you, write a design brief.

First, bad cover design

Here are examples of a few very common mistakes that you should avoid like the plague. These ideas scream self-published and hint, often unfairly, at the quality within.

- *Small boxes and lines.*
- *Badly placed fonts, or using too many fonts – 3 is a good maximum.*
- *Over long titles or subtitles.*
- *Poor image quality: the use of low-quality images that appear pixelated or blurry can be a major turn off for potential readers.*
- *Crowded design: a cluttered cover can make it difficult for readers quickly to understand what the book is about.*
- *Irrelevant images: the use of images that have little or no connection to the content of the book can mislead readers or leave them confused.*
- *Inconsistent branding: the use of inconsistent fonts, colours, or design elements can make it hard to establish a clear and recognizable brand for the author or book series.*
- *Overuse of effects: such as drop shadows or gradients can make the cover look dated.*
- *Lack of originality: over-reliance on clipart, stock imagery or design templates can make the cover look unoriginal.*
- *Poor colour choices: such as clashing or muted colours, can make the cover look unappealing or difficult to read.*

Our first cover concepts

As if to prove that cover design can be a tricky beast this one has been our most difficult one yet. How do you suggest all crafts and creative endeavours on one page? The answer finally came to us… you don't. Before that decision we created 3 fairly attractive designs each with their own serious drawbacks.

We asked my patrons and friends for their honest opinions.

Concept 1: A swirl of different crafts into a book.

We had some really beautiful pieces of art. The problem was they didn't hang together or say anything. They were attractive to the eye but my patrons found them confusing. They didn't express what the book was about.

2: This was a clever concept given to me by a friend. The idea was to suggest books and crafts together with the device of a bookshelf. This one got the most positive votes but I was never really comfortable with it. When we showed it to a designer he called it "scary" and suggested that it was "designed by the marketing department", which of course it was … us! We showed him concept 1 and he said it wasn't much better.

It was a shame that in the end we didn't put any of the wonderful artworks from the makers on the cover as every one was worth seeing so we put them on the inner leaves.

3: We then tried the concept of adding more chaos. It was the least popular most people calling it cluttered, although a couple of people said it was exciting to the eye, and it was Frank's favourite and he had input from the designer so we knew it was close. Its biggest problem is that it didn't say what the book was about, no matter how many crafts or how many page images we added to it. I'm afraid I hated it.

Also neither it nor the others sat well alongside the other book in the Your Creative Business series.

4: Shows the first iteration of a concept that balanced well with the Your Creative Business book. This is important if your book is or will be part of a series. The first design was made using Canva clip art. Frank hates clip art but some people make successful covers with it. If you are on a very tight budget it can provide a way of making a cover; at least to concept stage.

The final cover that made it onto the book blends the concepts of creativity splashing into a book, free-hand paint brush style, with the multiple pages of my books as a wallpaper in the paint. There are faint additional books on the side and the whole brush sweep is slightly suggestive of both a question mark and an "abracadabra" sweep of the creative arm.

Whether you prefer one of the other covers or not, you did buy the book so we might have got something right. In conclusion: if you can afford a designer you might have fewer headaches.

A typical "bad" cover design from a first time designer. An unoptimised image in a block, badly positioned text, and an "ugly" font

Initial cover attempt in Canva

Final cover design in InDesign

Looking back to a previous project, our self written brief for Your Creative Business was based on looking at the market. I had just bought one of Joanna Penns books called Your Author Business Plan. "A very empty, spacious feel. White background. Simple image."

Why? Because research into the genre of self-learning books has shown me that this style is currently popular with the public, and through my own buying habits I'm attracted to simplicity. Also younger creatives are no longer seen as "knitting grannies".

To get my first ideas through to Frank this time for the first time I decided to use Canva. With Canva you can play around with designs yourself and then you can send it to a professional for the important balance etc.

If engaging a professional for the final design, first look at other books in your genre. What are they currently doing? Don't copy anything but the general concepts. Colour/spacing, style etc. Then find someone whose work you like and ask what they think. You might find you have more of a feel than you think.

Your ideas will make the job quicker for the designer if you have one, and therefore cheaper for you.

In the end our cover still went through several iterations with Frank tweaking it to get closer and closer to something that would grab the customer's eye more than my first idea. We changed the name after finding out there was another book of the same title. I didn't like the colour or the font. It was too vintage.

By the way we are not designers and we would have passed it over to a designer if we'd been able to afford it. I'm sure a proper designer would be worth a couple of hundred to do the tweaks. You can actually change the cover design later when the book starts to sell. As long as your first book cover doesn't actually lose sales! I think my first one would have lost the younger and non vintage market. As a fairly old lady I didn't want to project that the authors were stuck in time!

Cover with an array of images formed around an oval. The oval is removed and the markup boxes do not show in print.

We have learned many painful lessons. Cover design is unforgiving in many ways but can be worked around by simply getting a very strong image and putting the title and author over it.

If you can't represent the book with a single image, use a collection of images formed into a shape. For instance in the moulding book we placed an oval in the centre of the page and aligned images touching all around it and one in the centre. Once the oval is deleted the eye still registers it.

An important question before laying the first element of a cover - is there room for text on the spine? Printers recommend not to try with less than 100 pages. Even then the text may be tiny below about 200. Calculate spine size using an online tool for your printer (Amazon or Ingram have them) and font size accordingly. You may need to leave as much space either side of the text as the bleed size, this is the accuracy printers work to and they will be likely to reject anything too tight to be sure of a good result.

Space all elements exactly, preferably use ratios to position them. The golden ratio 1 to 1.618 is often ideal but difficult to achieve. However 8:5 or 5:3 is good enough. These are well known by designers to be "comfortable".

Leave enough breathing room between spine, outer edges and bleed margins, or your cover title may be cramped when you get the print copy back.

The main text that needs to be on the cover is the title often at the top, a smaller subhead if any, then the author at the bottom. If you are tempted to put more than that think it through carefully. Maybe put it in a shaped box or circle. Any "loose" text around the cover could be distracting.

The back cover lets you highlight the main point in the book with accompanying images, however you must read the specification on how much space to leave for the barcode and exactly where.

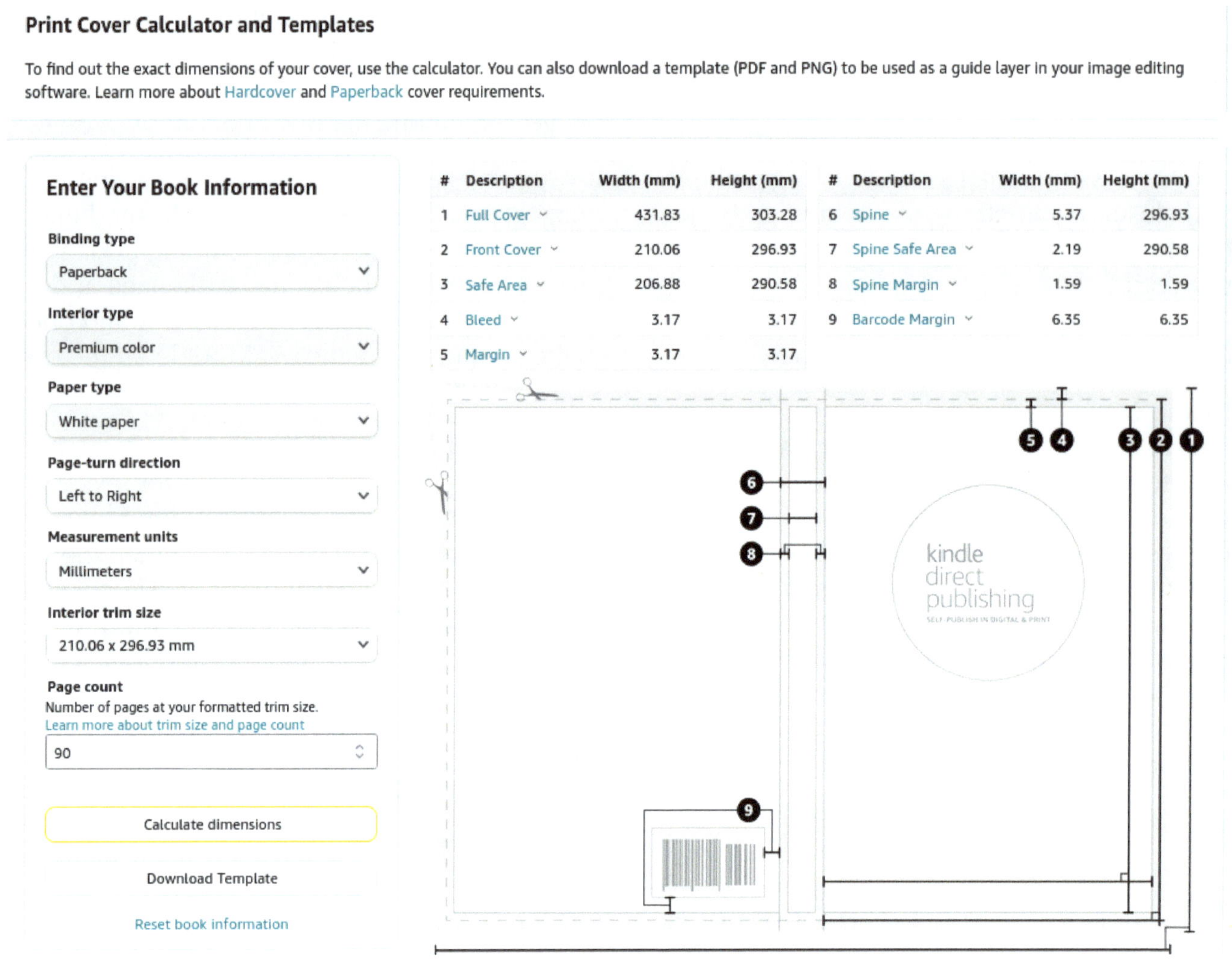

Print Cover Calculator and Templates

To find out the exact dimensions of your cover, use the calculator. You can also download a template (PDF and PNG) to be used as a guide layer in your image editing software. Learn more about Hardcover and Paperback cover requirements.

#	Description	Width (mm)	Height (mm)	#	Description	Width (mm)	Height (mm)
1	Full Cover	431.83	303.28	6	Spine	5.37	296.93
2	Front Cover	210.06	296.93	7	Spine Safe Area	2.19	290.58
3	Safe Area	206.88	290.58	8	Spine Margin	1.59	1.59
4	Bleed	3.17	3.17	9	Barcode Margin	6.35	6.35
5	Margin	3.17	3.17				

Enter Your Book Information

- Binding type: Paperback
- Interior type: Premium color
- Paper type: White paper
- Page-turn direction: Left to Right
- Measurement units: Millimeters
- Interior trim size: 210.06 x 296.93 mm
- Page count: 90

Amazon cover template generator - **https://kdp.amazon.com/cover-calculator**

Use the online tools to find the exact page size & bleed, printers will reject documents that are much more than a hair's thickness out. This can be very frustrating.

Finally the order to create the cover is the back page is the left half, then possibly a spine, then the front cover right half. Not always obvious on your first attempt.

Finished cover with barcode, design assistance from Michael Fitzmaurice

Part 9: The publishing process

Upload

At some point with Print On Demand you have to send your (hopefully final) PDF files up to be judged by the robots and staff before choosing pricing and distribution.

PDF files

Carefully check your entire book manually. No, not proof reading as the author really won't do that well enough – best to have another pair of eyes for that.

You can however do an overview - flick through checking things like page numbers and margins and pictures with bleed off the page all stay in the right place. Sometimes when you insert a page the software fails to notice. This means moving all the page fixtures and margins. It doesn't happen often but it has happened to me in the past, and I only caught it when flicking through just before uploading.

Make sure all your major headings are consistent (did you choose to not have a full stop then put one in a couple of them?).

Just make sure on the overview that it feels right and nothing jumps from page to page.

Make sure you have kept within the file size limits too, so don't fiddle with the default quality output settings as the CMYK print process is complex and relatively low quality so you won't normally get better results for sending more pixels.

Keywords / phrases

If you have made keyword lists (page 48) choose the best 7 key phrases, which will be entered here.

Categories

For Amazon you can have 10 (2 initial, 8 added later) for Ingram it is 3 initial. These can be important in getting extra sales.

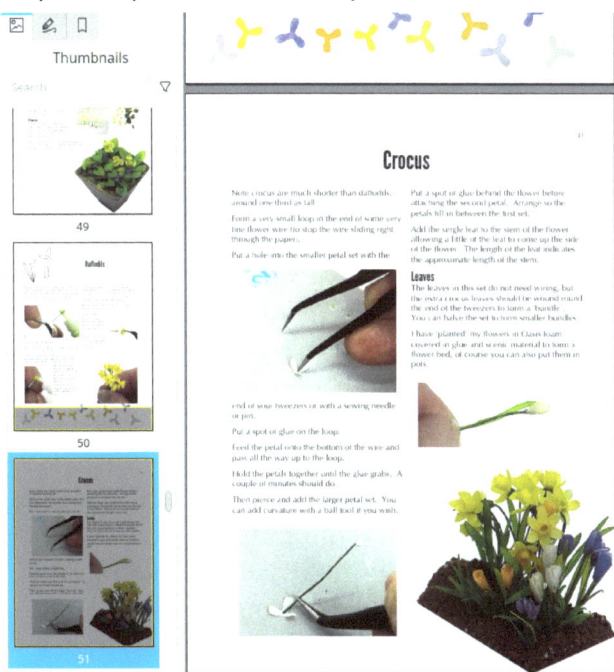

PDF checking of the book

Entering keywords, categories, descriptions into KDP

Descriptions

At this point you should already have a full description which will be visible to the customer when they click on your book's image on Amazon for example. You will also need a short one for Ingram which is used directly underneath search results, and for you to post on social media etc.

Pricing

We gave a brief idea of how to price earlier in the book, so hopefully by now you have used the online calculator from your chosen printer to calculate how much you will get for the book at your chosen price.

Next we tweak the various currencies to look nicer (e.g. 16.99 instead of 17.13 etc.).

Watch carefully at this stage as different countries may add different tax rates and you can choose to just accept it or tweak the price to the next obvious step up.

There are some currencies that we have no idea of the value of. Go to Google and check exchange rates to be sure it is a reasonable return in Australia or Canada for example as by default Amazon simply converts your US dollars price with no regard for extra printing costs country by country.

Expanded distribution

This gets books into bookshops and online retailers so it is worth looking at who gives the best deal if you are using more than one POD service. We choose to use Ingram for this as some independent bookshops are actively against using Amazon.

Entering pricing per country into KDP

Problems

Don't expect to get through the entire writing, layout and upload process with no errors. The companies change their requirements regularly. For instance on our last book the 'robots' insisted my bleed setting should be 3.2mm. In the past it was 3mm as default in the design software but it has now been changed to the US measurement of 3.2mm (1/8th inch). They have also done some small changes to the standard page sizes that they accept. I just ignored them and got away with it so far. Be ready for changes at any time.

Exact sizes for PDFs

To stand any chance of uploading to Amazon you must use the 'Print Cover Calculator and Templates'. This will tell you the exact sizes needed to 2 decimal places. And yes, they will enforce those to at least 1 place.

Error about exact cover measurements in KDP

On the plus side it will give you a template for the cover, margins, bleed, spine, spine text gap, barcode gap etc. This will save a lot of guesswork and refinement. The template is just as useful for any other POD service. You can place this PDF on a custom sized page and work over it, finally removing it when you are finished. See the cover design section.

Layout software crashing

This was a plague in the early 90s and still can happen today. Don't push your software to handle more than a few pages per document if they are loaded with images. Don't expect the software to be fast and stable if you also added automatic shaping to the text wrap for images over multiple pages.

Backup

Because of potential crashes, if you intend to spend weeks creating and setting a book with hundreds of images make sure you have a system in place from day one. I have an external drive that I back up to, and I set it up to never delete a file, ever. Instead it is copied to a folder on the date it was changed. So if you make a massive mistake on the Tuesday before you upload, then backup at the end of the day you can still go back to that folder on Wednesday instead of crying bitterly at the loss of weeks of work. Run the backup every day you work. Even a 32GB USB stick should hold everything you need if you structure your folders well. If you fill it, get another one.

Amazon versus Ingram

The advantages of Prime versus independent bookshops.

A hands down winner for anyone with Amazon Prime is the quick and often free delivery. Having checked this year's (2023) postal costs it would cost us over 10 euros to send a book to the US from here and with inevitable delivery delays of at least a week creating customer complaints etc. Quite a significant factor to account for. Even without Prime their local printing and delivery network keeps costs down.

Recently, profit margin is better with Amazon than Ingram for some countries but this may change.

Independent bookshops and many readers boycott Amazon however, and for this we also supply via Ingram. There is a small additional cost for this of an ISBN and Ingram setup fees. However, realistically, there are only a few weeks in the year when Ingram don't have free uploads available. We usually wait for the next free code to appear in their emails.

For ebooks the Kindle Unlimited scheme demands exclusivity with Amazon but pays a good rate per page read, sometimes even better than the sale price of lower price ebook. You can publish "wider" to Kobo, Smashwords etc. but we don't.

Proof copies

However perfect you think your finished book is, it isn't. Spend the extra week or so to get a proof copy printed and sent to you before setting the book for public release. It is amazing what things jump off a printed page when you have had a week to ignore the project. When editing you often see what you believe is there. When the proof comes you can see the mistakes you missed with the benefit of time and space. Maybe little things like misalignment, or even big mistakes like whole missing or repeated sections.

Publish your book just before payday!

One more thing. The timing of your publication can affect how quickly you get into the rankings. If you publish your book just before or around payday at the end of the month, that's a very good way of ensuring most of the people who said they would buy will actually buy immediately, sending your book rocketing up the rankings.

Congratulations!

You're an author! Please let us know if you've published a book with our help. We'll try to help give your marketing a push if we can.

Ebook

An ebook takes a completely different mindset than a print book. Put aside thoughts of controlling the layout and choosing fonts as it is better to let the user impose their own fonts and sizes to make it comfortable for them.

The internet is full of PDFs pretending to be ebooks but the format is an absolute nightmare for this use, especially for older people.

You need to think of a good ebook as text with images. The images are likely to be displayed full screen without the accompanying text. Don't dictate columns as many users will be using a phone or tablet in portrait mode.

Compatibility - Epub V2

Aim for an older standard like Version 2 as it will work on any device. Realistically a craft book won't need bells, whistles, animations etc. so it is easier to completely avoid the newer standards. Also Fixed Layout really isn't suitable for reading on smaller screens. Note you get this option only at the time of saving the EPUB, choose 'EPUB reflowable'.

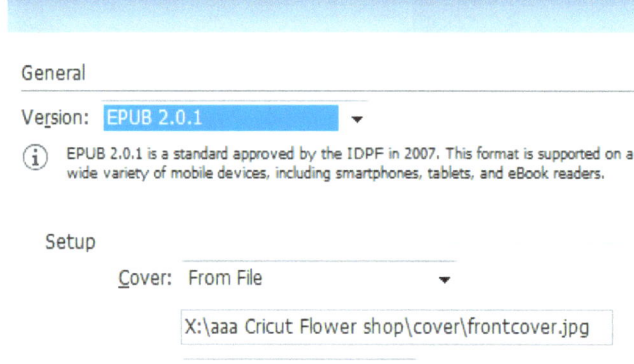

InDesign export to Epub V2

Shrink and compress images

I batch process all the images to a maximum of 600 or 800 pixels on the largest dimension. That is plenty for a small screen such as a Kindle device.

I convert PSD and PNG images to JPG as a matter of course.

Add a JPG compression setting of 60-70% to your whole image folder using a free tool. This is still more than good enough on a Kindle screen and saves a lot of space.

> Don't put high definition print images in as they are very large and Amazon can charge a fee based on filesize.

Using Indesign

InDesign has a handy 'Export Book to EPUB' function next to the 'Export Book to PDF' menu. I find this creates a handy starter for the ebook. Obviously with complex layouts and captions it can't get perfect results so careful hand checking is necessary, moving image declarations or captions around. The good news is it makes an excellent job of the awkward bits like creating the manifest and table of contents.

To edit and view the EPUB simply unzip it to a folder. EPUBs are just zips of HTML and images, so a standard text editor will let you cut and paste the image declarations around until you are happy, and your web browser will display the results for you as if it was a website.

After edit just add the changes back into the EPUB zip overwriting the old copies.

I found I had to tweak a few things to get the ebook how I wanted in terms of image size and resolution but it takes just 2 mins to do a full run so it is well worth getting it right. I choose Format: JPEG, Resolution: 300 PPI, Image Quality: Medium. I also opted to not include fonts as that can annoy people with a font preference already set or accessibility needs.

EPUB checking

Get your ebook perfect before uploading it and getting errors from Amazon etc. For this there are free checkers available that run on any computer.

The W3C web standards body released epubcheck which is very thorough. In fact, in my opinion excessively so. The spec was designed in 2007 but still highlights spaces in filenames which might end up generating pages of non-errors and hiding any real problems.

On the other hand Amazon's Kindlegen, though now obsolete, can still be useful as an initial check that you have all the images and files referenced in the EPUB without giving you spurious warning messages.

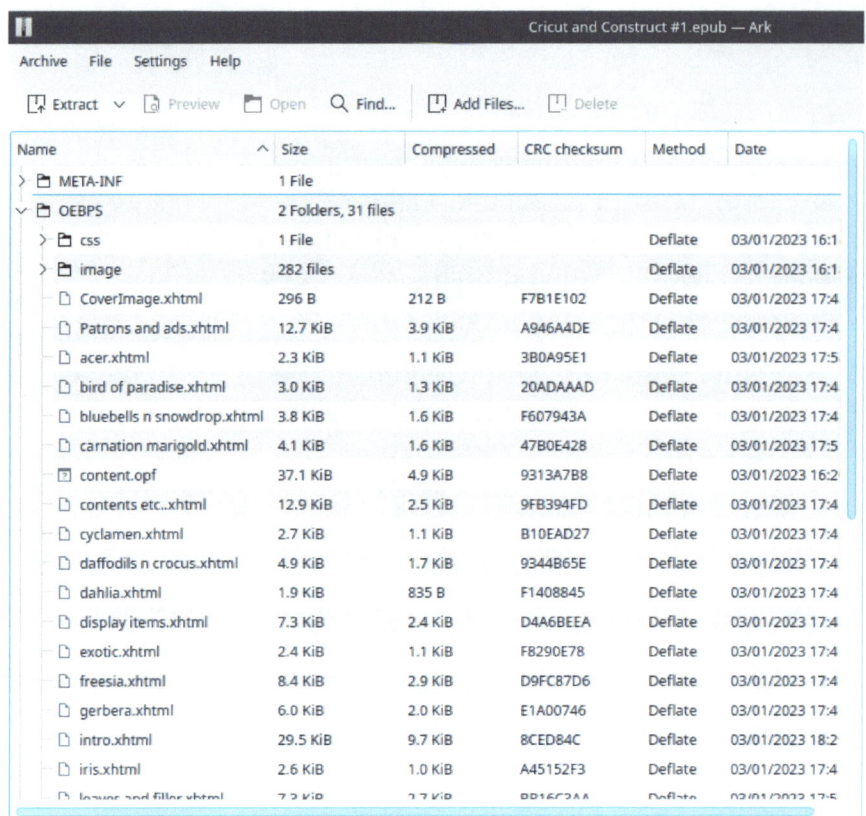

Contents of an Epub file

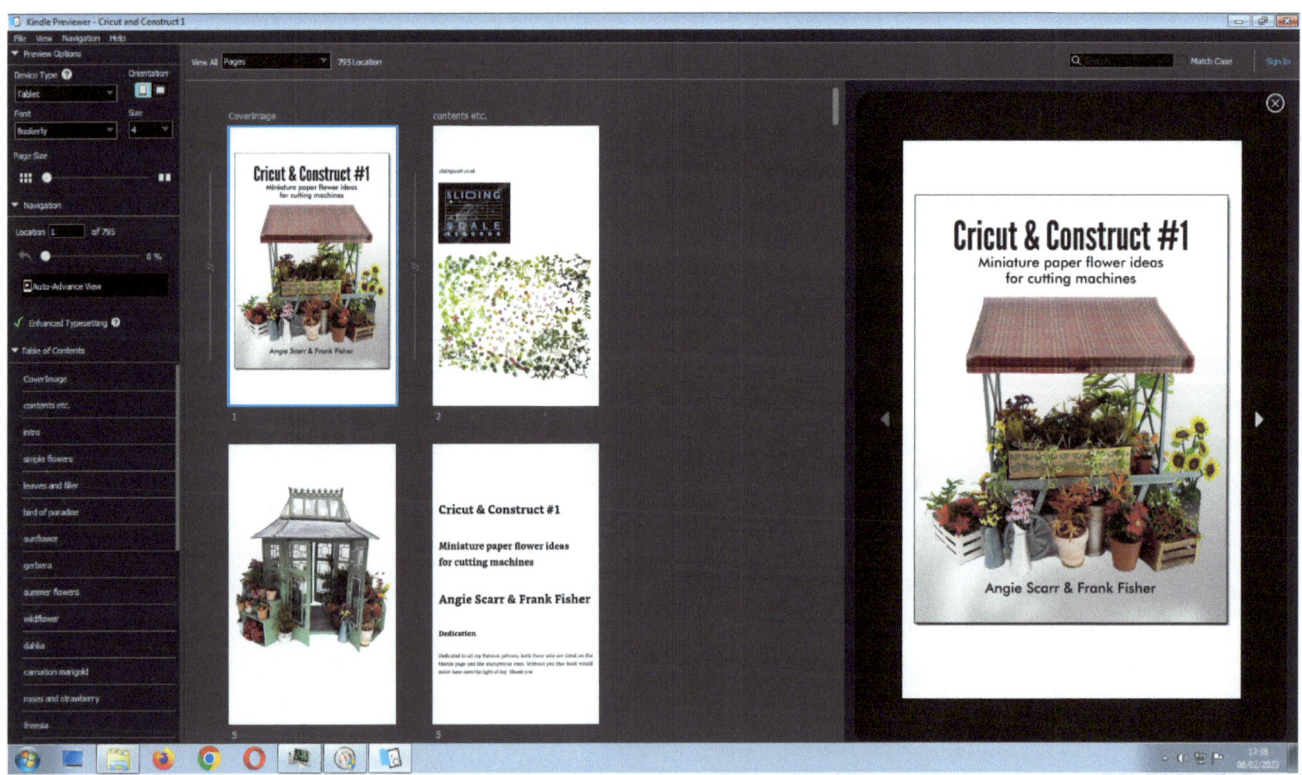

Kindle Previewer

```
****************************************************
Amazon kindlegen(Linux) V2.9 build 1028-0897292
A command line e-book compiler
Copyright Amazon.com and its Affiliates 2014
****************************************************

Info(prcgen):I1047: Added metadata dc:Title         "Cricut and Construct 1"
Info(prcgen):I1047: Added metadata dc:Date          "2022-12-23"
Info(prcgen):I1047: Added metadata dc:Creator       "Angie Scarr and Frank Fisher"
Info(prcgen):I1047: Added metadata dc:Publisher     "Frank Fisher"
Info(prcgen):I1047: Added metadata dc:Subject       "Paper flowers"
Info(prcgen):I1047: Added metadata dc:Rights        "Copyright (C) 2022 by Angie Scarr and Frank Fisher. All rights reserved."
Info(prcgen):I1047: Added metadata dc:Description   "Miniatures, 12th scale, paper flowers, Cricut, Silhouette, Brother, laser cutter"
Info(prcgen):I1002: Parsing files  0000029
Warning(htmlprocessor):W28001: CSS style specified in content is not supported by Kindle readers. Removing the CSS property: 'max-width' in file: /tmp/mobi-b0hEw0/OEBPS
Warning(prcgen):W14010: media file not found  /tmp/mobi-b0hEw0/OEBPS/frontcover.jpg
Info(prcgen):I1015: Building PRC file
Info(prcgen):I1006: Resolving hyperlinks
Info(prcgen):I1049: Building table of content      URL: /tmp/mobi-b0hEw0/OEBPS/toc.ncx
Warning(prcgen):W14016: Cover not specified
Info(pagemap):I8000: No Page map found in the book
Info(prcgen):I1045: Computing UNICODE ranges used in the book
Info(prcgen):I1046: Found UNICODE range: Basic Latin [20..7E]
Info(prcgen):I1046: Found UNICODE range: Latin-1 Supplement [A0..FF]
Info(prcgen):I1046: Found UNICODE range: General Punctuation - Windows 1252 [2018..201A]
Info(prcgen):I1017: Building PRC file, record count:    0000030
Info(prcgen):I1039: Final stats - text compressed to (in % of original size):   50.44%
Info(prcgen):I1040: The document identifier is: "Cricut_and_Construct_1"
Info(prcgen):I1041: The file format version is V6
Info(prcgen):I1031: Saving PRC file
Info(prcgen):I1033: PRC built with WARNINGS!
Info(prcgen):I1016: Building enhanced PRC file
Info(prcgen):I1007: Resolving mediaidlinks
Info(prcgen):I1011: Writing mediaidlinks
Info(prcgen):I1009: Resolving guide items
Info(prcgen):I1049: Building table of content      URL: /tmp/mobi-b0hEw0/OEBPS/image/stencil group 2017-07-_fmt.jpeg
Info(prcgen):I1017: Building PRC file, record count:    0000044
Info(prcgen):I1039: Final stats - text compressed to (in % of original size):   47.76%
Info(prcgen):I1041: The file format version is V8
Info(prcgen):I1032: PRC built successfully
Info(prcgen):I5000:  Approximate Standard Mobi Deliverable file size :    0009261KB
Info(prcgen):I5001:  Approximate KF8 Deliverable file size :    0009287KB
Info(prcgen):I1037: Mobi file built with WARNINGS!
```

Text output on an initial Epub check with Kindlegen showing title, author etc. and no errors
You can normally ignore the warnings here only actual ERRORs are a problem

Once you have generated the Epub, definitely use an ebook reader such as the free Kindle Previewer to check through every page and jump around in the table of contents. Simple errors such as listing the chapters in the wrong order won't show up until you do.

Check you have shrunk and compressed the images enough – an EPUB using 90MB will probably look no better than one using 20MB unless it is a huge amount of work – ours will be 100 print pages and under 20MB as an EPUB. You are likely to be charged for the difference. This could also inconvenience the reader as they may not have much space on their device.

Spelling errors on ebook

Amazon will spellcheck your ebook, which it doesn't do with the print version, and mark your book as lower quality if there are errors. So do your best to make sure there aren't any. Even so, often 2 or 3 words will be highlighted at upload and you can choose at that point to tell Amazon, one by one, whether they are a real error or not. You can go back and correct them in your ebook documents (and also in your print version too if it is a genuine error).

File sizes on ebook

There aren't realistic limits on upload of the ebook, just hidden costs if you don't compress carefully. Kindles all have a fast "email ebook" option to send it to your Kindle device for checking, but email providers will rarely allow more than 25MB.

Part 10: Post publication marketing strategies

Yayy! You have your final book. Maybe its not in your hand. Maybe you couldn't wait to hit publish after the proof corrections. It doesn't matter, you can still get going.

Marketing your book needs to be a prime slot in your day for the first couple of weeks. If you publish and forget your book will not sell even if it's really good. It took me a year to start marketing my The Frugalist book and guess how long it took to start selling? A year and a bit. Now it sells an average of one book a day which is not a fortune, but it's increasing. Another of my books I still haven't really got to grips with marketing and it really doesn't sell although it's a good book (in my opinion). You really have to believe in your book to market it well. If you let it slide, you have to ask yourself why. Why don't you believe in your own book?

Make a marketing strategy

This is not the time to sigh deeply at all the effort you put in, and take a rest. Just the opposite.

Get out your marketing strategy book. If you haven't got one … get one. It should already be full of names of people who said they are looking forward to seeing your book.

Never underestimate the importance of early sales to push your book into the rankings and get it noticed. Even without using Amazon's advertising Amazon will start to push your book to look-alike customers for other books in the same categories. So the moment you hit publish start mentioning that you have done so, and ask again who would like you to send them a personal message when it appears on Amazon. Create a buzz by asking people to tell you when it appears in their country. When it does appear, get back to every single one of the people who said they were interested in your book telling them it's available now. Ask them to let you know when they ordered it and where. Make a fuss of your first buyers in each country. They are your best friends and book selling allies. Cherish them! This can help you track when your sales will appear in the rankings and find the best of those. We found because the categories are better in North America than the UK we tend to show up first in Canada. It has a smaller pool to dive into so you can be a bigger fish earlier. This works for us meaning we can report high rankings early. This can create a real buzz around the release. Look at your Amazon rankings. If you get even higher in "hot new releases" this is the variable to push on social media for example.

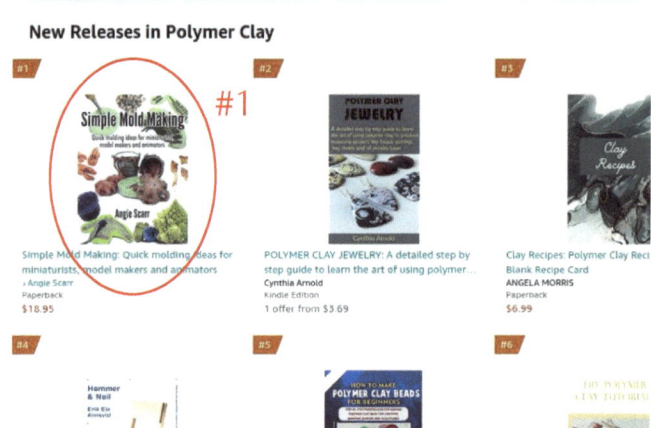

Ask your buyers to let you know when their book arrives, even to send you a photograph of themselves with your new book. And don't forget to ask them if they will be reviewing the book. Absolutely your most important sales are your first sales and absolutely your most important reviews are your first reviews.

Leverage book reviews: positive reviews can greatly influence a reader's decision to buy a book. Request reviews from book bloggers, online book clubs, and other relevant outlets.

To be candid, personally I'm a bit slack on review begging and there is one thing I've learned to be aware of.

Note that your lovely fans will want to say they're your friends/fans in the review. Discourage that, as both Amazon and the public are wary of that kind of review. Encourage honest reviews, not "I'm his/her friend" reviews.

I understand there are ways of whipping up more reviews but I'll leave you to look up those ways elsewhere. Those are outside my knowledge or experience. I do prefer natural and organic reviews. That said, most people need a few to start off with and need to encourage more. On my To-Do list is 'add a request for reviews in all the backs of our Kindle books'.

Virtual launch party for our Simple Mold Making book

Host a virtual launch online. We've done this a couple of times and they do work. Maybe do a little project online while your audience is looking in, chatting and asking questions. You can sign a bookplate for them if there is any interest in that. Get them to bring a bottle or a coffee and take a photo of themselves raising a glass or a mug to your book's success. This can be lots of fun in itself and people will look in on the video later for the free additional project or information.

I have already mentioned that some suggest that you offer book giveaways and that I'm not a big believer in this for craft books. Your fans will want to help you make your first sales especially if you've brought them along the journey with you. Giving away a book is another one that won't add to the sales figures or to the reviews. I have a couple of exceptions to this. You can buy copies of your book at full price to give to magazine editors, if you can afford to do so. Your sales will be registered and you may get magazine reviews. Of course on full price sales you get some of that money back.

Ebooks: It can be a very good idea to do occasional ebook giveaways to massage up interest. Ebook readers will often want to buy the physical book and giveaways do, I believe, register as sales. Our re-launching of the Frugalist book included a fairly large giveaway of free ebooks.

Carry on engaging with your audience: tell the world how excited you are that your book is here. Respond to comments and questions about your book on your social media accounts, and participate in online discussions related to your book or topic. Building an engaged audience can help generate interest and sales over time.

Keep in mind that marketing strategies should be tailored to your book and audience, and may require ongoing testing and optimization to achieve the best results.

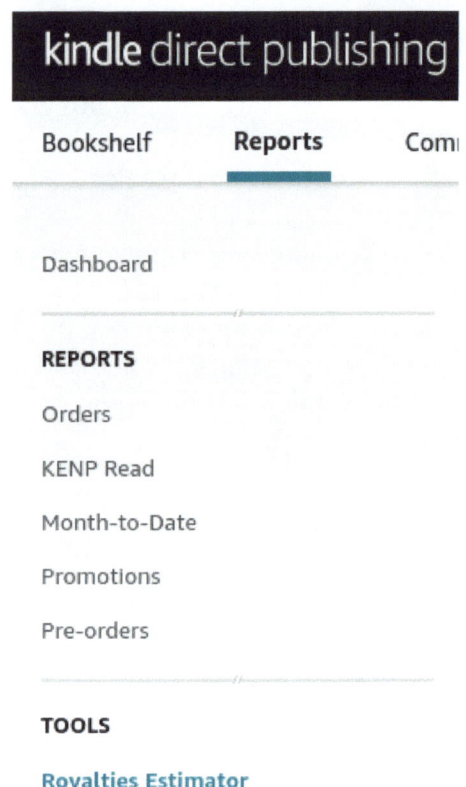

From KDP click on Reports then Royalties Estimator

There are several different ways of looking at your figures my favourite is the book comparison bar chart but that doesn't tell you day by day how much is print vs ebook vs K.U. reads.

Watch your sales appear on KDP

By the way, don't expect book sales to appear the day your customer orders. We believe it's the day the printer hits "print" or even "send/post". That seems to us normally to be the next day, however it may take a couple more due to weekends and national holidays. If this seems a bit hit and miss, remember your European books can be printed anywhere in Europe depending on which printer has the capacity that day. Your American books could be printed anywhere in the Americas.

So far I don't know where Australia and Asia's books are printed, it may be Victoria, but I imagine there will be a flow between countries 'down-under' too!

When you write your first book it all might appear very daunting indeed, and the results might seem disappointing. This is often down to reading too many books that offer you 6 figure incomes from the get go especially if you buy their courses/services. I do know that some of these people really do know their stuff and depending on what you can invest, some of them may well be worth buying. My advice if you want to go this route is buy their books on the subject first. Check out their free tutorials etc and decide if their teaching style resonates with you, but please, for goodness sake, ignore the marketing hype. Those who get lots of great ratings for their books are clearly doing something right. If only advertising. You can learn from them.

Check out Dave Chesson (Kindlepreneur), Joanna Penn (The Creative Penn), Mark Dawson and of course ALLi (the Alliance of independent authors). The membership of ALLi is a bit expensive for those on a shoestring budget but they also do books you can buy that cover a large chunk of the author journey.

Unusual activity

Radical dips can appear when there's a holiday, or a commonly used printer is experiencing high numbers or an outage. You will usually see only Kindle sales and reads on these days but they are usually followed by a high peak when the printers get back online.

Since national and religious holidays and 'sabbath' days can be different, you can expect the sharp edges on sales figures to become a bit fuzzy. However it's pretty fair to extrapolate from your figures once you get used to looking at them in a certain way. For example on the 21st of Jan below you see a very wide mix of book sales. Over the few days before that I'd been tweaking my Amazon advertising across all the books that appeared. The spread of different books which sold on the dates 19th, 20th & 21st is interesting and probably related to the advertising. Earlier good sales were residual xmas sales. Late January and February can be improved by advertising which is why I changed the Amazon ads at this point.

Because reports seem to be made when a book is actually printed and ready to go, when you see sales coming in on your KDP royalties estimator go and have a look at your rankings on the various countries you're selling in.

For us Monday and Tuesday seem to be slow days on reports of book sales suggesting that Sunday and Monday are slow book sales days.

Backing up your books / tutorials with video

I know for certain that video boosts book sales especially if you get a vid about your work onto a popular Youtube channel or a popular TikTok. Whether these channels are yours or those of a popular friend or even someone you're collaborating with, doesn't matter. I really hate doing video if I'm honest but it is by far the cheapest and most effective sales tool. I can map my sales on the 'compare books' function on our KDP sales estimator and see where a big leap occurs. A lovely jump in sales on my book Cricut and Construct happened recently when my friend Lisa Sones-Peck put out a little video looking through my book. It was just a really short vid but it sold a good few books, that much is obvious.

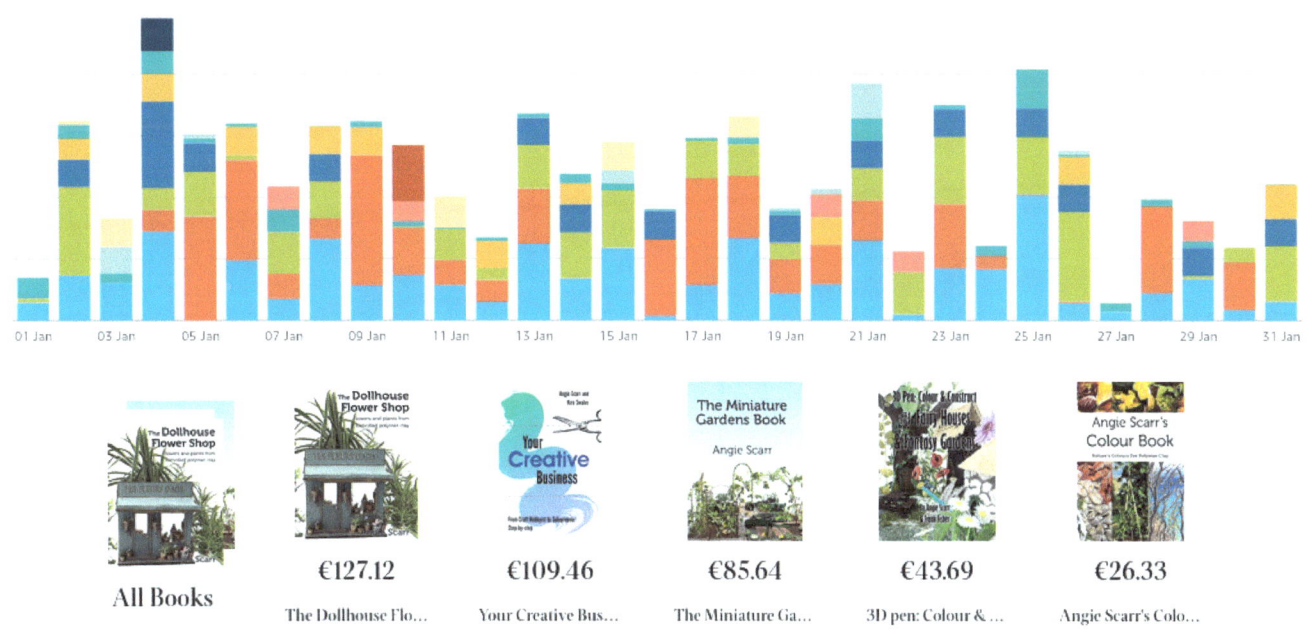

Check your Amazon rankings

Best seller rank - the BSR calculation more heavily weights recent sales. But people who have tried to crack the actual code used by the ranking engines have failed to do so. This may seem like a bad thing but really it's good for small businesses like ours because it gives us an equal shot at having a best seller. There are however some hints and tips which are more likely to get your book selling well right from the off.

The most important thing to remember is that people don't hear about you until you tell them. Then they may hear about you from Amazon or from readers' feedback but as I keep reminding you, your first sales are the most important.

Canada is ultra fast both reporting and shipping and since sales are currently lower overall it's easier to rank in the busy craft categories, so your Canadian customers are your best friends if you want to be able to say 'Bestseller'.

The image below is the the Best Seller list as we found it today. Fortunately for us for the writing of this book our Cricut book appears as #6 and our friend Lisa's book is also there in Most Gifted. Grab a screenshot whenever your book ranks well (we forgot) to use in your advertising. This is an especially good idea when chatting on social media.

Requesting extra categories

One of the most important of your post publication marketing strategies is category adding. Many self-published authors don't know that you can add quite a few more categories to your book which will gauge where they show up and help you to get ranked. I believe you can have up to 8 more category paths.

You will perhaps have noticed that some books in certain categories seem totally random. It can be very annoying to find low content books or books with no relevance to your categories splattered all over the top slots. But you still have to play the game. And you should not fall into the cheeky way they do it which is find categories that are easy to rank in and put your books in there. Find relevant categories and correct paths to them. If you don't send the correct path to Amazon your request could be denied. That said, many of us wish that they would check a bit more carefully.

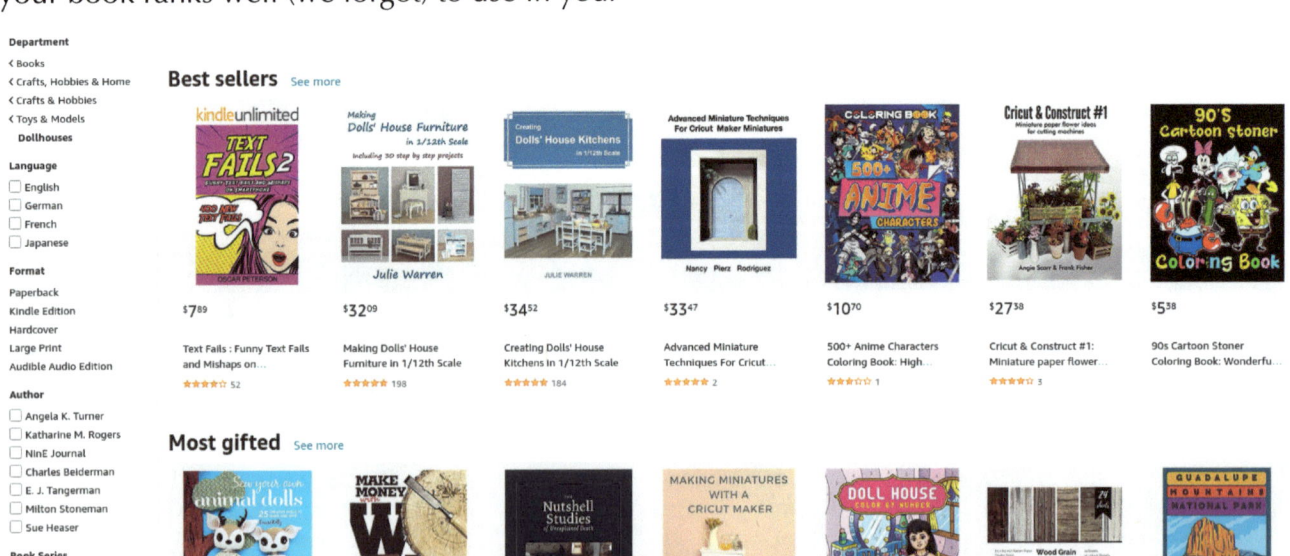

ASIN: B0BQDSS21H
US print

Books > Crafts, Hobbies & Home > Crafts & Hobbies > Toys and Models > Dollhouses
Books > Crafts, Hobbies & Home > Crafts & Hobbies > Toys and Models > Miniatures
Books > Crafts, Hobbies & Home > Crafts & Hobbies > Toys and Models > Toymaking
Books > Crafts, Hobbies & Home > Crafts & Hobbies > Toys and Models > Models

ASIN: B0BRL97JLD
CA Kindle

Crafts, Hobbies & Home > Crafts & Hobbies > Miniatures
Crafts, Hobbies & Home > Crafts & Hobbies > Toymaking
Crafts, Hobbies & Home > Crafts & Hobbies > Models
Crafts, Hobbies & Home > Crafts & Hobbies > Papercrafts

Category paths

Above are examples of good paths. Please be careful and check each category exists for each country listed otherwise your entire request is bounced back to you. Even between US, Canada, Britain and Australia there is no consistency at all. And even worse the Kindle categories are different to the print ones in many cases.

Amazon Ads

The dark arts of advertising

Unless you are intent on a "hot launch" (see page 50) you may find this section too challenging for now. You can ignore it until the book is finished. We didn't even know about it for our first book. We have a section on recovering from a slow launch later (see page 92).

Glossary of terms

ASIN: Amazon Standard Identification Number. It is a unique identifier assigned by Amazon to products they sell. This will be in addition to your ISBN

Impressions: refers to how many times Amazon shows the target audience your advert. You need at least a couple of thousand impressions to get an accurate idea of whether your ad is reaching anyone at all and if they are the right people.

Clicks: how many people clicked on that ad. If you dive deeper it will be how many people clicked on that exact target. Always remember clicks aren't sales. If clicks result in a good percentage of sales then you have a great keyword/product target. Normally however, you can expect about 10 clicks per sale so set your bid accordingly. Between as low as possible and 1/10th of what you are prepared to pay for each sale.

CTR: Click Through Rate, What percentage of people who have potentially seen your ad have actually clicked on it to read further.

Spend: total amount you have paid for the clicks in the selected time period.

CPC: Cost Per Click. How much you have paid on average for each click. This can vary if you have set extra potential increases/decreases.

Orders: how many books you have sold in that period.

Sales: how much money those orders have made - as total cover prices of books.

ACOS: Advertising Cost Of Sales. Always remember that ACOS is not the cost of gaining your part of the selling price of the book. So, depending on what proportion of that book sale is your profit you really want to keep down to 25-30% of sales as a limit. It may go over from time to time if looking at a shorter period of time but remember it's not a daily thing. A click today may result in an order that doesn't show up on your sales figures for a couple of days.

Target(ing): which keywords or products you have chosen to advertise alongside.

In its simplest terms Amazon ads chooses to deliver an icon image of your book to people who are browsing for other books or

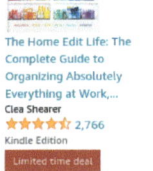

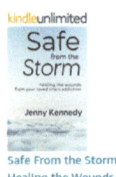

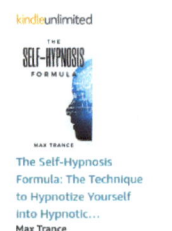

Sponsored products (Amazon ads) related to "The Frugalist"

products under related keywords or when they are looking at those books and materials. It appears Amazon will first deliver you a set of books (or products) where your keywords are the closest to the title or subtitle. But when you pick from that list and look at that book/product, underneath it will deliver you 'related' adverts. If you look above the photographs of the related books, some of them have a flag in the top right hand corner that says 'Sponsored'. That means someone is paying to show you the book.

When targeting your potential customers, you want to bring them to and help them decide to buy your book, either instead of, or as well as the book they were originally looking at or for.

It's easy to be confused and even afraid of Amazon ads because it looks like you have to spend a lot of money and the fear is that your ad will suddenly run ahead and spend more money than you had intended or can afford. I advise setting your daily spending limits low if you're a newbie. Amazon has that little notice that tells you most people opt for a minimum of 10 euros/pounds/dollars a day. Take that with a large pinch of salt as most of us little people don't! Don't be put off or belittled. Set your limit at a dollar or two a day and forget it. Amazon will tell you if you have reached your limit and you can go and see if there has been any success so far that might make you want to raise your limit. However don't expect instant success. Expect to spend a month or two just trying things out.

Do not be pushed into spending too much because of FOMO (Fear Of Missing Out) All that said if you really want a hot launch and want to spend more in the early days by all means set a limited term at a tenner a day. It's your money and your belief in your book.

Along with very many authors I highly recommend Dave Chesson's videos. I wanted to use his "Publisher Rocket" to help me with my ads but it wouldn't work on my operating system. No worries, they refunded me immediately so it's a brand I trust and would go back and buy again once they get it working on Android. Because there is so much information out there on Amazon ads for novels and nonfiction I'll skip straight to my experience and say that I'm no expert. There are experts who claim to make most of their income through advertising but be aware. Yours is a niche market so you really have to drill deep into it for success. Remember, Amazon is always changing things. They seem to level out at an advertising cost per sale of around 20% of selling price which of course is a large chunk of your cut. I have had lower and higher ACOS percentage but that has been my median. We like to use Amazon advertising for the books that bring in sales of my ancillary products.

How to set up your ads

If you want to get into detail on Amazon ads we can recommend free courses from Kindlepreneur **kindlepreneur.com/free-amazon-ads-course** and an extensive set of courses, resources and tips from Amazon **advertising.amazon.com/en-us/resources/library#1**

Amazon will also send you invitations to register for online courses provided by their trainers.

We are not experts and the above provide good free advice on going deeper into the system. We are only going to offer a basic walkthrough and some of or experiences.

First, open an advertising account
Go to Create Campaign
This will be in blue. Probably in the middle LHS of your screen.

Go to Sponsored Products
(sponsored brands is not relevant for your first book)

I personally would never use lockscreen ads because I find them intrusive and they can actively put me off an author, at least in the short term. For that reason I can't give you any more information about them, but Amazon will explain them if you click on it just to look.

You then have a choice of custom text or standard. That means you have the choice to say something short about your book that will grab the people you're trying to attract to your book. This week you might want to say "This book will change your way of thinking about sea glass and inspire you to create stunning pieces". You might decide to change your ad later to "create beautiful jewellery with one of the most beautiful recycled products in the world".

Choose which products (books) you want to advertise
I'm still playing around with whether to add the ebooks to my products to advertise. If I don't advertise them with the paperback book will I lose sales to ebook readers? If I do, will I get more clicks for too high a price because I choose to keep my ebooks very cheap. I think this is a blunt tool for this reason.

Keywords IS | IR	Match type	Sugg. bid Regular days	Add all
electronic books IS: 0	Broad	$0.14	Add
	Phrase	$0.20	Add
	Exact	$0.79	Add
make electronics IS: 0	Broad	$0.18	Add
	Phrase	$0.61	Add
	Exact	$0.69	Add
muscle car book IS: 0	Broad	$7.14	Add
	Phrase	$0.49	Add
	Exact	$0.59	Add
world cup book IS: 0	Broad	$0.51	Add
	Phrase	$0.52	Add
	Exact	$0.81	Add
graphic design IS: 0	Broad	$0.59	Add
	Phrase	$0.54	Add
	Exact	$0.36	Add
classic car book IS: 0	Broad	$2.29	Add
	Phrase	$1.67	Add
	Exact	$2.07	Add
train books adults IS: 0	Broad	$0.66	Add
	Phrase	$0.60	Add
	Exact	$0.75	Add
polymer clay jewelry IS: 0	Broad	$0.18	Add
	Phrase	$0.20	Add
	Exact	$0.35	Add
dover mathematics	Broad	$0.58	Add

Hopeless and expensive automatic suggestions for the Simple Mold Making book

Automatic or manual targeting

With Automatic targeting Amazon decides on the search terms used. Sometimes they are on point but often they are wildly out, especially in the case of nonfiction and craft publications. Normally you don't want to spend your money on getting clicks from people who are just curious. Of course sometimes you do! If you want to raise awareness of a completely new genre that might be exactly what you want.

Product or keyword targeting

Product targeting
Will often be by other similar books but in the craft genre may also be the materials used so for my 3D pen book I might target another similar book (there weren't any when I wrote my first) in which case collecting the ASINS (Amazons sales item number) of those books is good.

You might also collect product numbers for related products. For my 3D pen book that was pens, filaments, mats and templates. I chose to leave out templates because the sort of people who would buy templates would be less likely to buy a book IMO. They might, however, click on my book out of curiosity, and cost me money.

Keyword targeting
Using the words people might use to look for books similar to yours.

For example If you have written a craft book in a similar genre to one you have seen you can target that authors name as a search term keyword or the actual book by entering it as an ASIN. Or words contained in the subtitle or description. If your bid is successful Amazon will show your book alongside or underneath the book your potential customer is currently looking for or at.

Select: Manual Targeting and then Keyword Targeting

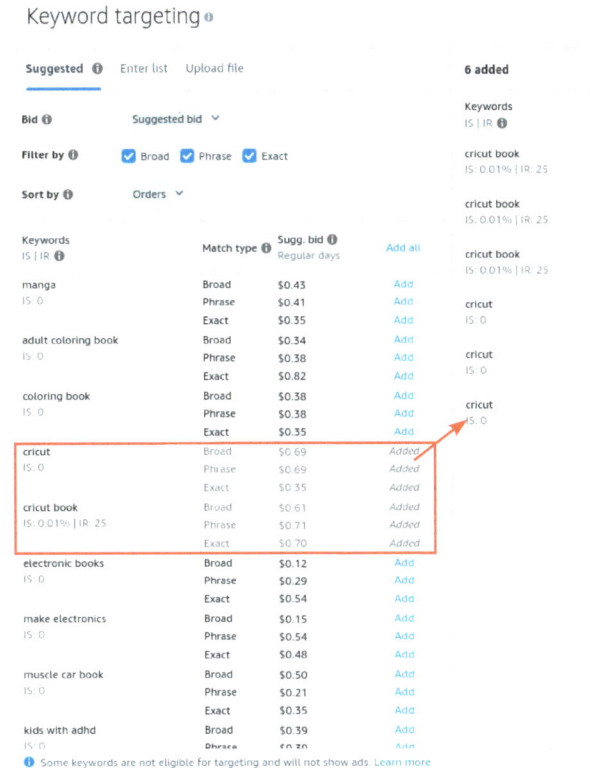

Manual keyword targeting

Write in key phrases that people might be using to search for a book exactly like yours. Those phrases might well be at the top end price-wise.

Default bid
I always set my default bid VERY low to start. Where there's a suggested bid I tweak the bids after I've entered them

Spending limits
Personally I set my spending limit very low. I'm not a person who is very much affected by FOMO and I know Amazon will notify me if the adverts are getting lots of clicks and I need to revisit my spending limits. If that happens you can up it but watch the conversion rate closely for a few days because they may not convert instantly to sales, Equally they may not convert at all in which case you might want to tweak those search terms

Expensive search terms/ product targets

It is my opinion that you shouldn't pay for expensive search terms unless your book is very new and/or in a totally new genre to you

An expensive search term is likely to generate a lot more visibility, a lot more clicks and a lot more expense but will it generate sales? It's likely to, yes, BUT what you might be doing is paying for people to take your books. If your ACOS is over about 30% you know you are paying more than you are getting. Let's take the example of "cricut book : exact" at 70c. Ten clicks are likely to result in one sale. Your ACOS would be $7, you would probably lose money selling a standard priced book. See the explanation of ACOS on page 86.

Fast start advertising using expensive but popular search terms is better for pushing a book to gain sales figures (rankings) and reviews. You may get better early sales figures and get to a good place on the bestseller lists and make Amazon, and the public, notice that your book sells. Until writing this I've never tried this tactic as it seems a bit 'cheesy' however I do now have a book that's outside my usual genre and in a potentially big market so, for the purposes of research, I'm going to invest a few euros in a quick blitz-advertise.

This would work best if you ask for reviews and ratings in the back of the book. Asking for reviews works best in the Kindle versions because your reader is already holding an electronic device.

Cheaper advertising

Remember, you only ever pay for clicks; not for sales. So, what I call "mining for unconsidered relevance" is my favourite strategy for long term campaigns that you can

Keywords IS | IR	Match type	Sugg. bid Apply All	Bid	
model vegetable IS: 0	Exact	-	$ 0.02	×
model vegetable IS: 0	Broad	$0.80 $0.50 - $1.00	$ 0.80	×
model vegetable IS: 0	Phrase	$0.88 $0.70 - $1.05	$ 0.88	×
models and maquettes	Broad	-	$ 0.02	×
models and maquettes	Phrase	-	$ 0.02	×
models and maquettes	Exact	-	$ 0.02	×

Remove "broad" and "phrase" to leave "exact" at 2c

ignore for months at a time. It is certainly cheaper. Check once a month for any runaway successes or failures. If your ACOS goes over 30% you are probably losing money; but not necessarily.

Using "keywords" from the ad menu, allow it to give you any keywords it thinks you might use. Choose any from that list that you really want to use. You'll note that they may be expensive. Add them anyway and then choose to use them at that bid. Or you can lower the bid in case you get lucky and someone else's bid runs out. Or as I do, you can try using similar phrases that someone might use if they articulated themselves in a slightly less mainstream way. You can find 60 of these in an hour easily and x3 (broad/phrase and exact) that's a lot of potential keyphrases. However they will be very rarely used so expect to wait a year for one click on each! Here's an example:

When I was looking for keywords relevant to my Your Creative Business book I found "passive income business ideas" was taken but "passive income business book" was not … Kerching! I bid just 2 cents on that.

"Craft business book" expensive … "craft business ideas" … not. "Soap making business book" exact 2 cents. I nabbed that. "Soap making business book" as a phrase - 54 cents minimum bid. I chucked that one out.

"Solopreneur success" expensive, "successful solopreneur" 2 cents. "Photography business" expensive "photographer business" 2 cents.

Obviously the ones that are expensive are likely to be keywords that are used most regularly. But not always. I'm looking for those elusive people who are looking for a book about their particular craft, or a book about running a business in their particular craft. If the first group aren't quite ready to run a business they are certainly pretty likely to think "Hmm, I wonder if I could make money from this" so they are certainly a potential spontaneous buyer. Because it's a bidding war you can always find undiscovered relevance that other people have not thought of.

Good bad-spellings!

As this world seems to get less literate, look for the most common spelling mistakes or typing slip-ups. The various bad spellings of polymer clay miniatures are my current faves!

Because this is a long term strategy you are likely to have slower results. The delivery of those ads is very sparse but it's very precisely targeted at the people who have entered those exact words or phrases and so when you do get a click it's a low cost but the likelihood of a sale is very high especially if the phrase is pretty obscure but very relevant. I've had ACOS on this method of one or two percent BUT you don't get many sales this way. You do however catch people who are really looking for your exact product and who are more likely to review it well.

If you want to get rich quick, this way you won't, but this is a nice long slow burn on book sales and if it yields results that boost your book sales for a lowish cost it can carry on rolling as Amazon starts to push your popular book anyway. They know it makes sense for them. You can do a lot of time consuming work on keyword finding websites such as Moz or you can just play around. After all, if nobody clicks on it, it costs you nothing.

Do make sure you save as draft regularly so you don't lose any work that you've done within the platform.

Negative keywords might be necessary if you have a book that could be confused with other genres, or words in your title that could lead to confusion. For example if you had a book about Millefiori caning you wouldn't want people to come for the wrong reasons and you might want to exclude the word punishment etc. I have only ever used negative keywords on one of my campaigns. I excluded "fungus" in my moulds book ads.

I mentioned that ACOS is really important and that normally you shouldn't allow it to go above 30% but don't forget there may be that raising of awareness which comes within the price but doesn't show up as direct sales. People could see your book on advertising one day but go in weeks later under a different search term, find your book again and buy it because at the back of their mind your book now has some authority. Readers could see one of your books and decide not to buy that one, but another of yours. This wouldn't show up as a sale and your ACOS would stay high but this might mask sales outside the advertising that was triggered by the ad. Of course this is only important when you have more than one book. It's possible that Amazon will decide not to deliver ads on these keywords if they don't produce sales easily.

Launch campaign

Then when you are happy you have filled in every field hit Launch Campaign and wait for them to approve. Your first approval might take a day or even 2 but I've found mine can go live very quickly indeed. It seems you reach a "trust level" after a few campaigns. I might be wrong about that though.

Keep an eye on your ads

Especially any new ones, to check if your advert is working. Open the specific ad by clicking on the title of the campaign. Go to targeting on the right side. This will open the search terms you have put in. Set it to whichever parameters you are most interested in. Often this will be clicks, sales and ACOS at first.

Look again at which of those clicks result in sales. Eliminate those that don't to save money. You can go deep into your targets and eliminate those that get clicks but no sales.

On the slow burn campaigns leave for a long time. All the experts agree that you need to leave campaigns going for a good long while to see results. With my low cost slow burn strategy even more so. But If you're doing a hot launch and prepared to pay big to get the book into as many hands as possible you'll have to be more careful about it running away.

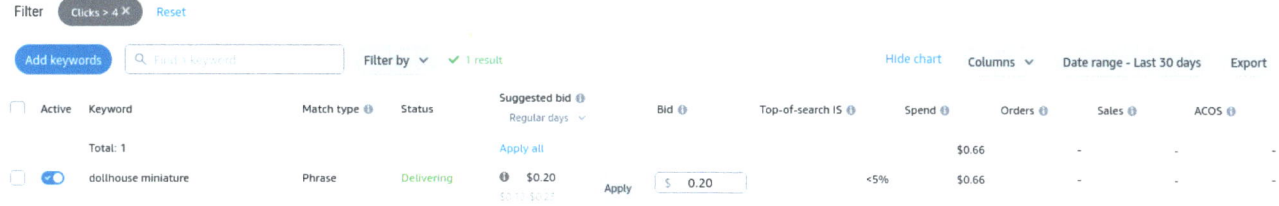

"dollhouse miniature" accounted for most of the spending on clicks on the Cricut & Construct book

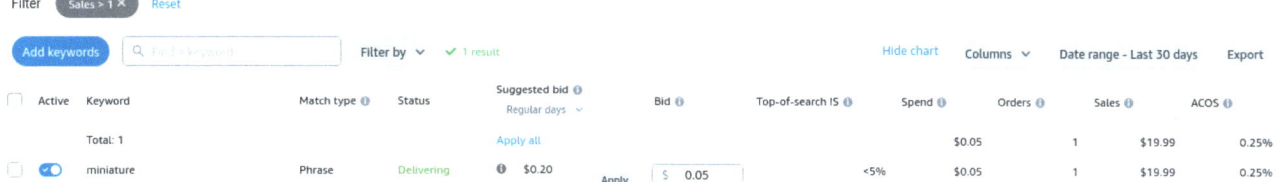

but "miniature" got the sale, possibly people searched for dollhouse but didn't have the Cricut machine

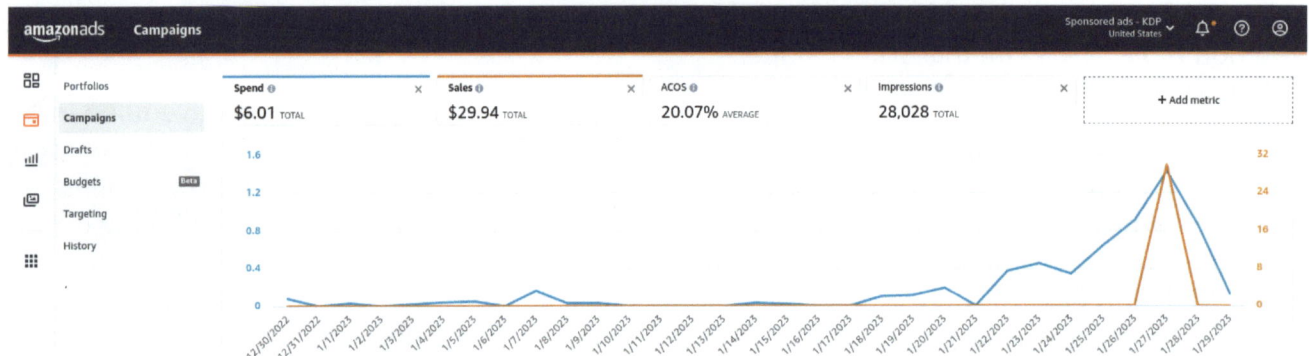

Advertising related spike in sales

Advertising leading to sales elsewhere

If you publish through Ingram Spark as well, your customers may choose the Ingram version if it's cheaper so, if you have that under a different ISBN, it might be that you gain sales from an ad that don't go reported in the Amazon ad sales. This will mean your ACOS can appear high for the number of sales you actually do make. This could happen pretty regularly where people are looking for a cheaper deal and the Ingram buyers are essentially drop-shippers who advertise but don't buy until they have an order. So do keep an eye on your Ingram sales whenever you have an important campaign running in case your sales there do very well out of it. This might mean that you don't mind having a slightly higher ACOS as you know the sales are registering elsewhere.

Another reason potentially not to mind a higher ACOS is if people are likely to buy other related products from you after buying your book. Two of our books have that. In one case we kept the book price really low so that the customers don't mind paying for it, in another case we kept it high and are prepared to spend more on advertising. The target buyers of this second book generally have more disposable income and are unlikely to quibble about the price. So price and marketing style have many variables.

Here is a screenshot of when I spent a long time on a very tiny expenditure, then decided to add some more campaigns and some more money. You can clearly see the difference. What we don't know is if the low spend was generating interest in my books as a whole if people went away and bought a different book or bought through Ingram Spark.

How to come back from a cold or failed launch

I have had a few slow launches. This is because inside my very hardworking exterior, there sits a very lazy toad. I brought my "The Frugalist" back from the dead by opening a Twitter account and tweeting about politics and frugal living. I really enjoy that. To be honest, because it's a side of me I used to have to reserve for trusted friends and family but now, as I get older I can let the "Littleoldladywho" out! I've also given more ebook copies of this book away than of any other book and the power of the giveaway shouldn't be ignored. After all, you are mostly giving to people who might not have tried it without. If you know most people will like and appreciate it, it's a very good way to get reviews and ratings. You have to imagine you are launching again and find your ideal readers and where they live. Now that book sells more copies than any of my other books. I was making less income out of it because at the time I was deliberately underpricing. It has taught me that if you put enough effort in, a dead title can be revived. I wrote this one because I knew people needed it. I revived it because they need it even more now. I recently put up the Kindle price to 2.99 from its former 79 cents/pence. Strangely, even frugal people seem to value the book more since I raised the price a little and I have actually sold more copies. I know it will save people a lot more. As a frugalist myself, I'm very aware and grateful that it buys me a frugal meal a day and now, to be fair, I would rather it bought both of us a meal. So if your book is not selling:

Check the following:

- *Check that you have the price set to an appropriate price in the market but not too low*
- *Try re-designing the cover and relaunching*
- *Check the format is appealing. Is the book the right shape and size for the market?*
- *Check that your description is impactful and shows that it meets the needs of potential readers*
- *Take some time to distil the niche readers and look at the potential for a wider market*
- *Let magazines and podcasters etc. know what your book is about and how it will interest their listeners. Join journalist mailing lists like HARO*
- *Try a free ebook giveaway to encourage reads and reviews. Make sure you market the giveaway as thoroughly as if it were making you money*
- *If you are not on Kindle Unlimited consider putting your book on Unlimited before the giveaway. During the free promotion you may also get paid reads on Unlimited*
- *Have a relaunch party or do a video a podcast or a blog about the work including a live demo*
- *You can't officially change the title but you can put a new subtitle or flash info on the book cover*
- *Ask your friends and fans to give advice about the book.* **Ask for reviews!**

Frank and Angie both wish you the very best on your writing and publishing journey and, because we're both creatives and building our own author business alongside other multiple income streams, we're very happy to publicise your book once it's out. We know how little pushes can go a long way so please let us know if you're in the process of writing a book or are actually publishing. We'd also love to hear if this book has helped you and about anything you think is missing, or any information you find to be incorrect or misleading. Please do review this book if you have the time; rate it if you don't.

And please feel welcome to join the following Facebook groups:

www.facebook.com/groups/selfpubauthors

A very small select group of self-published craft authors and would-be authors.

www.facebook.com/groups/yourcreativebusiness

A group for all those making their living or part of their living from crafts, or those who are considering starting a small craft or creative business.

Biography

Angie Scarr's greatest love and therefore her skill, is in solving three dimensional problems, finding short cuts and sharing them with the miniaturist and crafting world. Angie is better known for her innovative-at-the-time techniques in polymer clay which are now part of the way miniatures are routinely made. With 30+ years experience in the craft world Angie has now moved on to business coaching through her books and Patreon.

Keeping it all together is her slightly younger husband, Frank Fisher. Frank is a self confessed "computer geek" who has many years of experience in solving problems for artists, craftspeople and musicians, helping them realise the digital part of their dreams. Frank is now running Angie Scarr Miniatures at their self built home in rural Spain where they live with their two cats Smoosh and Squirrel.

For more biographical details and some of Frank and Angie's crazy adventures see the blog on www.angiescarr.co.uk/blog and Angie's autobiographical book Making It Small, available on Amazon as a paperback or ebook.

Thanks and acknowledgements

Thanks to Kira who we constantly ask for advice! To Lisa Sones-Peck for constant support and encouragement of many kinds, for just being an all round thoughtful person and great fun to share inspiration and problems with.

My patrons without whom the past 5 years would have been much more difficult if not impossible and none of the last few books would have been written. You are all my supporting angels!

Christine McKechnie, Sue George, Grethe Holme Jantzen, Mandy Lancaster, Gill Bayes, Sandi Kluge-Smith, Karin Sørensen, Gillian Mason-Thompson, Jacquie Hall, Tara Jane Susie Langworthy, Karen Rollinson, Rachel Taylor, Lisa Sones Peck, Petra Sujiker, Denise Pinnell, Essie Kenneway, Maryse Cuypers, Stephanie Ryan, Roslyn Hill, Mary Katherine Myers, Michaela Wolzen, Fay Victoria Durrant, Marta Teran, Helen Cruickshank, Barbara Taylor-Harris, Dicky Lambregtse, Sandy Hadley and, of course, many more who didn't give permission to be named but who are just as important to us. Thank you all!

Reviews

Reviews really help self-published authors compete in the field. Please review or rate this book if you have time. We really appreciate every single review.

Let us know if you have published a book on Kindle Unlimited and we will happily review your book if we like it.

Patreon
Why I love my patrons

If you've never heard of Patreon before, imagine you could be a "patron of the arts" in some small way helping your favourite artists to continue working, inventing and teaching in their specialist area. Artists no matter how well known in their field often have no regular guaranteed income and in the past often gave away their inspiration for free because until micro-payment platforms there wasn't an easy method to gain an income from day to day teaching, support and skill sharing.

This subscription service is an easy way to connect artist teachers with their students and followers, and as a way for the patrons to give the level of support they are comfortable with and receive in return perks such as advance knowledge of really new ideas before they ever get to publication. Some ideas of how I made things which never even reach the books which I call my "daft ideas". They also get free SVGs and discounts on our website and membership of an exclusive Facebook group.

Many thanks to my current 70+ patrons some of who have been with me for several years now. You've all given me courage to start with new things like this book. The Patreon thing has really helped me because it's like having 70 sets of shoulders to lean on. 70 therapists and 70 special friends to share my daft ideas with and see if they work. Or at least are interesting enough for you not to walk away! 70 people who understand that no matter how well known an artist is they still may struggle from time to time. That's worth so much!

www.patreon.com/angie_scarr

Making Miniature Food & Market Stalls
Angie's first book published by Guild of Master Craftsman Publications. A bestselling introduction to making polymer clay miniature food. This is an updated edition.

Miniature Food Masterclass
Angie's second book with GMC. Also still a bestseller this one continues the journey of exploration into what polymer clay can replicate.

Other books by Sliding Scale

Simple Mold Making
A book full of quick molding ideas for miniaturists, model makers, animators and jewellers using 2 part (silicone) mold material.

The Dollhouse Flower Shop
This book concentrates on the innovative idea of stencilling flowers in polymer clay/liquid clay mix. Some equipment and materials are needed to get started.

The Miniature Gardens Book
Have you ever fancied making more than just a flower garden in miniature? Angie gives you several garden styles and lots of new ideas.

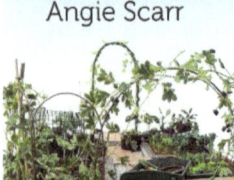

3D Pen #1 Fairy Houses and Fantasy Gardens
A handy pattern book for anyone of any age who is looking for a project to make with their 3D pen. Excellent addition to a 3D pen gift.

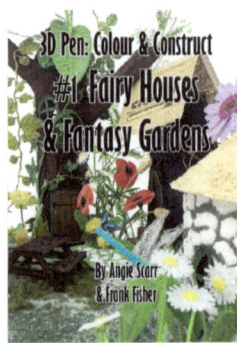

Your Creative Business & Workbook
Angie and SEO expert Kira share advice on all aspects of craft business from pricing and marketing through to multiple income streams to help you ensure a more secure future.

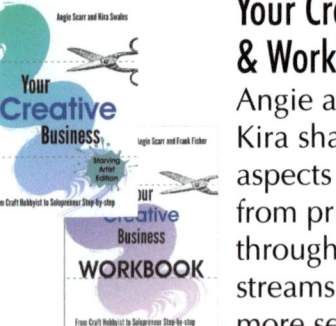

Cricut & Construct #1
Miniature flowers for Cricut and Silhouette machine users. Includes: design how-tos, cutting tips, painting techniques, assembly guides and display ideas.

Angie Scarr's Colour Book
New large edition book that asks the big questions about colour realism in polymer clay, helping you towards work that is so realistic it jumps out from the rest.

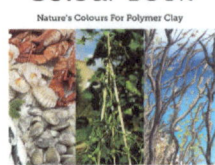

Angie Scarr Miniature Challenges Parts 1&2
Revisiting all the old magazine articles in Dolls House and Miniature Scene and other dollhouse magazines.

Making it Small- Biography
Angie never lived an "ordinary life". When she and Frank met it became less ordinary still. A story of the love of crafts, miniatures, self building and life in a small pueblo in Spain.

The Frugalist
A look at revaluing your time, living better for less and gently preparing for unexpected crises. If life sometimes feels tough this book might help.

Bladder Cancer Stories
A personal, often humour filled journey through the downs and even ups of radical cystectomy and chemotherapy: back to health and a different view on life.

Index

ACOS	86	Kindle Previewer	78
Amazon ads	86-93	Krita	53
ASIN	86	launch ad campaign	91
audience	14	launch party	81
author services	10-11,15,44	layout (cover)	67-72
backgrounds	26	layout (inner)	57-65
backups	21,75	lighting	27
barcodes	66	margins	59
bleed	58	marketing	36-42,48-52,80-93
body text	60	master page	58
captions	61	page size	57
categories	48,73,84-85	PDFs	73
co-operation	38	photo editing	53-55
colour balance	53	photography	26-29
colour levels	53	Photoshop	53
colour saturation	53	planning	12,17-18,20,23-25
columns	59	pricing	47,74
compress images	77	problems	22,74-75
contents pages	64	process shots	29
costs	10	profit	10
cover design	67-72	proof copy	76
cover template	72	rankings	84
cutouts	54	reader	14
default bid	89	research	13,37
description	52,74	sales reports	82
downloads	20,23	Scribus	56
dynamics	31	secrecy	38
ebook	77-79	self-pub companies	11
editing	43	spelling errors	79
end matter	44	spellings (for ads)	90
EPUB	77-79	spending limits	89
file sizes (ebook)	79	sponsored products	87
file structure	56,77	stylesheet	59
fonts	59-61	subheadings	61
front matter	44	subtitle	48
grammar checker	30,43	targetting ads	88
headings	61	text flow	61-63
hot launch	50	title pages	58
hybrid companies	10-11,15,44	titles	61
image resolution	26,77	upload	73
InDesign	56,77	USP	15
index pages	64	vanity press	45
ISBNs	66	writing exercise	31
keywords (phrases)	48,73		

www.angiescarr.com

For moulds, stencils, kits, books, miniatures and craft materials
delivery worldwide

www.etsy.com/shop/AngieScarrCrafts
Our Etsy Digital store for plotter/cutter files. Flowers, leaves, boxes and a flowershop are among the designs.

www.patreon.com/angie_scarr
Support me and get sneak previews of my work, free SVGs and discounts in our shop.

www.facebook.com/angiescarr.miniatures
My Facebook page where I let everyone know what is going on

www.instagram.com/angiescarr
Photos of work in progress

www.pinterest.co.uk/angiescarr
Links to my work all over the internet

ko-fi.com/angiescarr
Buy me a coffee

www.tiktok.com/@angiescarr
Video shorts

www.youtube.com/user/angiescarr
For tutorials, howtos and videos about crafts and miniatures